EDEXCEL A-LEVEL/AS RELIGIOUS STUDIES

PAPER 3 NEW TESTAMENT STUDIES

1   CONTEXT OF THE NEW TESTAMENT

Published independently by Tinderspark Press
© Jonathan Rowe 2018

CONTENTS

ABOUT THIS BOOK

This book offers advice for teachers and students approaching Edexcel AS or A-Level Religious Studies, Paper 3 (New Testament Studies). It concentrates **on Topic 1 (Social, historical and religious context of the New Testament)**.

The other topics are:

2 Texts and interpretation of the Person of Jesus

3 Interpreting the text and issues of relationship, purpose and authorship

Together with this one, these books cover the AS course or Year 1 of the A-Level; the remaining books cover the topics in Year 2 of the A-Level.

4 Ways of interpreting the scripture

5 Texts and interpretation: the Kingdom of God, conflict, the death and resurrection of Jesus

6 Scientific and historical-critical challenges, ethical living and the works of scholars

> Text that is indented and shaded like this is a quotation from a scholar or from the Bible. Candidates should use some of these quotations in their exam responses.

Text in this typeface and boxed represents the author's comments, observations and reflections. Such texts are not intended to guide candidates in writing exam answers.

CONTEXT OF THE NEW TESTAMENT

What's this topic about?

What is the setting for the New Testament? Where does it take place, geographically and historically? This unit looks at the background to the New Testament in the Jewish religion, the politics of the land of Palestine and the religious conflicts of Jesus' day.

1.1 PROPHECY REGARDING THE MESSIAH

This topic looks at the history of the **line of King David** and the **Suffering Servant** in the Book of Isaiah; it links these to the New Testament, especially **Matthew's 'proof texts'** which show Jesus to be the Messiah and the concept of the **"Messianic Secret" in Mark's Gospel**. **Raymond Brown** and **Morna Hooker** are the key scholars here.

1.2 THE WORLD OF THE FIRST CENTURY

This topic looks at the importance of **Hellenism** (Greek culture) and the **Roman occupation** for the Jews of Palestine as well as the different **Jewish sect**s formed in response to these influences. There are no key scholars for this section but the ancient historian Flavius Josephus is the main source.

Before you go any further...

... there are some things you need to know.

"WHO WROTE THE BIBLE?"

The Bible isn't one book: it's a collection of books by different authors, living in different places and different centuries. It's divided into two collections:

- The **OLD TESTAMENT** was written by Jewish authors, stored on scrolls and brought together as a complete collection some time around 500 BCE. The Jewish religion doesn't have a single authority to decide what counts as Scripture and what doesn't, so the collection is based on tradition. There are some books (scrolls) of the Old Testament that aren't accepted as Scripture by everyone.

- The **NEW TESTAMENT** was written by Christian authors (most of whom - perhaps ALL of whom - were Jewish before they converted to Christianity) over the period of about 100 years after the lifetime of Jesus - certainly all were written by 120 CE and some as early as 50 CE - for reference, Jesus was crucified in 30 CE (although some historians argue for 33 CE). Not all of the New Testament authors knew each other personally and we can only identify a few by name.

The earliest Christian writings are the **epistles** (letters) that the missionary **Paul** wrote to his Christian converts in Turkey and Greece and later to Christians in Rome. These letters were written in the 50s CE and early 60s, within living memory of Jesus.

The four Gospels that describe Jesus' life, death and resurrection come later. **Mark**'s Gospel is believed to be the earliest, probably in the late 60s CE; **Matthew** and **Luke** come later, in the 80s; **John**'s Gospel is widely believed to be the latest, in the 90s or early 100s CE.

> *As you can see, the people who knew Jesus personally were already old or dying when the first New Testament texts were written; most were dead by the time the later Gospels were written. You should reflect on how much you think this matters...*

The first Christians were Jews who believed Jesus to be their Messiah. Gradually, more and more **Gentiles** (non-Jews) joined the Christian community. These converts often had little understanding of Judaism. The biggest event for the early church was the **Great Jewish Revolt** of 66-73 CE. This ended when the Romans destroyed Jerusalem and the Jewish Temple. After this point, the Jewish Christians seem to have been rejected by their Jewish friends and relatives and the Gentile Christians broke off their connection with Judaism. Christianity and Judaism went their separate ways as distinct religions.

> *Most of the New Testament texts come from the period when Christians were figuring out their identity as a religion separate from Judaism. These writers were looking at Jesus' life, death and Resurrection with 'the wisdom of hindsight' and it coloured the way they describe Jesus and his dealings with the Jewish religion.*

"WHAT'S ALL THIS BCE AND CE DATING STUFF?"

For centuries, Westerners have followed the Christian dating system that makes the (supposed) birth of Jesus "Year Zero". All dates before that are **B.C.** ("Before Christ") and after it are **A.D.** ("*Anno Domini*" or "In the Year of the Lord"). This dating system is based on the Christian belief that the arrival of Jesus was the most important event in word history and a 'turning point' for the human race.

Other religions have their own dating systems. In the Jewish dating system, all dates are calculated from the Creation of the world in the Bible and are known as **A.M.** ("*Anno Mundi*" or "In the Year of the Word"). Islamic calendars are calculated from Muhammad's flight to Medina (the *Hijra*), which took place in AD 622 in the Christian calendar.

The fact that the world uses the Christian calendar is largely due to the spread of European empires and colonialism. However, scholars writing for a modern, multicultural world are moving away from a dating system based on such religious values. In its place, the terms **B.C.E.** ("Before the Common Era") and **C.E.** ("Common Era") are used. This is a sort of compromise that keeps the same starting point for the calendar but removes explicit links to the Christian religion.

> *Before you start grumbling about "political correctness gone mad", reflect that the BC/AD system wasn't invented until the 6th century and was only used by monks for the first 500 years - and that the BCE/CE system dates from the 17th century and has been used by Bible scholars pretty consistently - which is why I'll be using it and so should you.*

TOPIC 1.1 PROPHECIES CONCERNING THE MESSIAH

The idea of Jesus as the long-awaited Messiah is central to Christianity, but it's a complicated concept with some controversial views. Most Jews rejected the claim that Jesus was the Messiah they were expecting and continue to reject it to this day; Christians have argued that Jesus was a different TYPE of Messiah to the one that was expected.

What is Prophecy?

A **PROPHECY** is a message inspired by God. This means it is a form of **revelation**. A person who passes on prophecies is a **PROPHET**.

> *We're used to thinking of a "prophecy" as a prediction about the future - but as New Testament students you need to get over this misconception. Some prophecies predict the future, but many (perhaps most) are messages about the present. A big debate in New Testament studies is whether certain prophecies should be understood as referring to the future (**futurist**) or the present (**preterist**).*

Prophecies come in different forms:

- **Writing.** The Bible describes God giving Moses the Ten Commandments in written form

- **Through angels.** God used an angel to tell Moses the message he was to deliver to Pharaoh of Egypt (**Exodus 3:2-4**) and an angel told Mary about the birth of Jesus (**Luke 1: 26-48**).

- **Visions.** Visions sometimes happen while the prophet is awake (**Isaiah 1:1**) but others happen while the prophet is in a trance (**Acts 10:10**) or asleep (**Daniel 7:1**)

- **Mental guidance.** God guides the thoughts of his prophets to convey his message; this is the meaning of the Bible's statement: *"All Scripture is inspired by God."* (2 Timothy 3:16).

When Jesus spoke to a Samaritan woman, he revealed things about her past that he could have known only by divine revelation. She recognized him as a prophet even though he had made no predictions about the future (**John 4:17-19**). At Jesus' trial, his enemies blindfolded him, hit him, and then said: *"Prophesy! Who is it that struck you?"* They were not asking Jesus to foretell the future but to use supernatural power to identify who had hit him (**Luke 22:63-64**).

Because of this, Biblical prophecies are difficult to interpret. A prophet might be saying things about his own time - about kings and empires and moral problems for the society he was living in. However, readers years later find that the words of the prophecy seem to apply to them too. This is certainly true for the Old Testament prophets.

From a **PRETERIST** viewpoint, the Old Testament prophets are talking about:

- God's anger with the people of their own time for their sinful ways

- A criticism of the kings of their own time for failing to follow God's laws

- A warning that the rival empires of Assyria and Babylonia are plotting to overthrow the Jewish Kingdom

- A hope that a better king will come along to save the Jewish Kingdom from its enemies, rule justly and restore good religion

For example, Martin Luther King was often described as "prophetic" for his speeches about racism in America. He wasn't predicting the future, but he was telling the American public a deep truth about themselves and their society that they didn't want to here. This is what made him "prophetic".

From a **FUTURIST or HISTORICIST** viewpoint, the prophets are talking about:

- God's future destruction of sinners on Judgment Day

- Future empires that will persecute God's people (such as the Roman Empire or the Nazis)

- Predictions of Jesus as the future Saviour

Believers don't agree on how to interpret prophecy. Liberal believers tend to take a preterist view and treat the prophets as describing their own time and only accidentally describing future events; conservative and fundamentalist believers tend to take a futurist/historicist view in which the prophets (whether they realised it or not) were describing events centuries in the future. Of course, prophecies can do both: they can describe the present and the future.

A good example comes from one of the greatest prophets, **Isaiah**:

*For to us a child is born, to us a son is given, and the government will be on his shoulders. And he will be called Wonderful Counselor, Mighty God, Everlasting Father, Prince of Peace - **Isaiah 9: 6***

Sounds familiar? You probably recognise it from carol services - it's often read out at Christmas in churches

From a preterist perspective, Isaiah is describing the birth of a royal baby and hoping that the young prince will grow up to be a wise and successful king. From a futurist/historicist perspective, Isaiah is describing the birth of Jesus (700 years later) and predicting the arrival of the Son of God in a stable in Bethlehem.

Introducing the Messiah

The Messiah is referred to throughout the Bible as a chosen one of God who will come in the future to set the world to right and save God's people.

MESSIAH comes from the Hebrew word, **Mashiach**, meaning *"**the anointed one**,"* or *"**the chosen one**."* In Old Testament times, prophets, priests, and kings were anointed when they were given their positions of responsibility. This ceremony involved pouring oil into the hair and beard to make it shine. The anointing was a sign that God had chosen them.

> *In Europe, crowns were placed on the heads of kings and popes. In the British coronation ceremony, the monarch is crowned <u>and</u> anointed with oil, showing they have political and religious power.*

Over time, "messiah" stopped meaning **anyone** who had been anointed to be God's chosen leader - it started to mean a **particular** person who was chosen by God for a very special destiny.

Christos (Christ) is the Greek equivalent of the Hebrew term, **Messiah**. When Andrew met Jesus, the meeting was a sort of **religious experience** for him. He went to his brother, Simon Peter, and told him, *"We have found the Messiah"* (**John 1: 41**).

> *So 'Christ' isn't Jesus' surname. 'Jesus Christ' means 'Jesus the Messiah'.*

The Messiah is referred to directly or indirectly throughout the Bible. For example, **in Genesis 3: 15**, God describes how a descendant of Eve's will crush the Serpent who tempted humans to Fall. Many believe this to be the first reference to a Messiah. Later on, Moses tells the Israelites:

> *The LORD will raise up for you a prophet like me from among yourselves, from your own kinsmen* - **Deuteronomy 18: 15**

This was also interpreted as predicting the future Messiah.

Isaiah has many prophecies about the birth of a prince interpreted as predicting the Messiah (p32); **Micah** describes the Messiah as being born in Bethlehem (p34). Many of the **Psalms** (religious songs in the Old Testament) were interpreted as describing the Messiah.

Despite (or because of) all these references to the Messiah, Jews in the 1st Century had arrived at differing expectations about what the Messiah would be like.

THE KINGLY MESSIAH

Most of the time, the word "messiah" is used in the Old Testament to refer to a king and many Jews expected the future messiah to be a great king. In the 1st century, the Jews were occupied by the Romans and their supposed-kings were the sons of the hated King Herod the Great. In contrast to these pagan emperors and tyrants, the Jews looked forward to a true king of the **line of David** (p12) who would rule fairly and wisely.

Some looked forward to more than that. They hoped for the **occupying Romans** (p53) to be driven out of the land and the **publicans** (collaborators) who had worked with them to be punished - in other words, a settling of scores. These Jews hoped for a Messiah who would be a warlord who would smash their enemies and set up a Jewish state based on Biblical laws. The **Zealots** (p67) who waged guerrilla war against the Roman occupiers and murdered publican collaborators probably hoped for this sort of Messiah.

Some went further still, hoping for a supernatural king or angelic ruler who would defeat not just the evil empires of the world but the demons that controlled those empires. This Kingly Messiah would rule the whole world and abolish war and suffering.

The prophet **Daniel** describes the Messiah like this:

> *He was given authority, glory and sovereign power; all nations and peoples of every language worshiped him. His dominion is an everlasting dominion that will not pass away, and his kingdom is one that will never be destroyed* - **Daniel 7: 14**

THE PRIESTLY MESSIAH

In the 1st Century, Jewish priests worked in the Jerusalem Temple (p59), a vast building that had been enlarged by Herod the Great. Ordinary Jews had to pay taxes and other fees to bring animals for the priests to sacrifice there. The priesthood was seen by many as corrupt and collaborating with the Roman occupiers.

Some Jews looked forward to a messiah who would reform the priesthood, perhaps abolishing the Jerusalem Temple and setting up a better, holier form of worship that was accessible to everyone. The **Essenes** (p65), who lived in desert monasteries and rejected the whole Temple-cult, seem to have hoped for this sort of Messiah.

THE PROPHETIC MESSIAH

The 'Age of the Prophets' seemed to be over by the 1st century, but many Jews hoped for a great prophet who would guide their nation back to God. They lived in confusing times, surrounded by a pagan Hellenic culture, ruled over by the Romans and distrusting their own religious and political elites. Moses had promised that God would send another prophet just as great; this prophet wouldn't lead an army or build a temple but he would teach people how to worship God and be good Jews in these troubled times.

This view was probably popular with many ordinary people and with the **Pharisees** (p63), a religious sect that taught people how to live holy lives by following the Jewish Law closely in every detail of their private lives, rather than waging wars or sacrificing animals.

THE SUFFERING MESSIAH

This is a controversial idea. Christians claim that Jesus was (in a way) all of the above types of Messiah - a king, a priest and a prophet - but he was also a Suffering Messiah who died an **ATONING DEATH** (a death which makes up for other people's sins). There are passages in the Old Testament that seem to refer to a Suffering Messiah - most famously the **Song of the Suffering Servant** in **Isaiah 53** (p17).

These passages, written 700 years before Jesus, certainly *sound* like a description of a Suffering Messiah. The big debate is, was there actually a belief in a Suffering Messiah in the 1st century? If there was, then Jesus seems to fulfill this prophecy in very precise ways.

> *But if there wasn't, then the "Suffering Messiah" sounds like something Christians came up with later, so that Jesus would "fit the bill" for a Messiah after his unexpected death by crucifixion ruined their hopes that he was going to be a successful king, priest or prophet. We will consider this argument later.*

THE MESSIANIC AGE

All of these views united in the belief that the arrival of the Messiah would usher in a new age of peace on Earth. There would be an end to war - though this might be because a Kingly Messiah had conquered the Roman Empire or perhaps a Prophetic Messiah had taught everybody to be more peaceful. The Jews scattered throughout the world would return to Palestine to worship together. There would be no more suffering or evil.

Isaiah describes the Messianic Age like this and the role of the Messiah like this:

> *He will judge between the nations and will settle disputes for many peoples. They will beat their swords into plowshares and their spears into pruning hooks. Nation will not take up sword against nation, nor will they train for war anymore* - **Isaiah 2: 4**

And, even more strikingly, with this image of a world where all natural enemies - even carnivorous animals and their prey - are reconciled:

> *The wolf will live with the lamb, the leopard will lie down with the goat, the calf and the lion and the yearling together; and a little child will lead them* - **Isaiah 11: 6**

> *Jews today still await the Messiah: they look forward to OLAM HA-BA ("the world to come") which is the Messianic Age. Some Christians think the Messianic Age will begin with the second coming of Christ.*

OTHER MESSIAHS

After the death of Herod the Great in 4 BCE there were revolts among the Jewish population against his son (also called Herod!). Judas son of Hezekiah led one particularly bloody revolt; Herod the Great's ex-slave Simon of Peraea led another. Both men tried to set themselves up as Kingly Messiahs but their rebellions failed.

The Romans gave up on ruling Judea through a Jewish King and sent a Governor of their own instead. Naturally, there was a revolt against him too in 6 CE, led by Judas the Galilean and his Pharisee ally, Zadok. Judas was another failed Messiah but he did found the **Zealot** movement.

King Herod Agrippa (so many kings called Herod!) also declared himself to be the Messiah - but the Bible records he was stuck dead by God "*and worms ate him*" (**Acts 12: 23**). Flavius Josephus argued that his patron Vespasian was really the Messiah, after the Roman general Vespasian defeated the Jewish Revolt in 70 CE and became Roman Emperor - although Josephus admits that not many ordinary Jews viewed Vespasian that way!

About a hundred years after Jesus, the Jews launched a final revolt against the Romans. The leader was **Simon Bar Kokhbar**. Things went well at first and Bar Kokhbar expelled the Romans and ruled as a prince - he declared himself to be the Messiah and was recognised as the Messiah by the leading **Pharisees**. However the Romans returned in force, led by the Emperor Hadrian. The Romans destroyed the Judean state and massacred Bar Kokhbar's supporters - the Romans suffered heavy losses but half a million Jews were killed and more were sold into slavery and deported. Bar Kokhbar's dreams of an independent Jewish state - and a Kingly Messiah - died with him.

THE IMPORTANCE OF THE LINE OF DAVID

One of the most importance qualifications for someone to be the **Messiah** is that they are descended from the greatest King of Israel: **David**. The Christian claim that Jesus is the Messiah depends upon Jesus being the "*Son of David*" and descended from the Davidic royal line.

King David

David is (after Moses) the main hero of the Old Testament. He lived around 1000 BCE at a time when the Twelve Tribes of Israel were coming together as a kingdom. He began life as a humble shepherd boy from Bethlehem but was taken into the court of Israel's first king, Saul. When the kingdom was split by civil war, David led the resistance against the cruel Saul. After Saul was murdered, David became king. He founded the United Monarchy, ruling over all the Israelites. David made Jerusalem his capital and brought the Ark of the Covenant there to be a focus for the worship of God. His reign is looked back on as a 'Golden Age' of just rule and pure religion. David is a sort of ideal: a great warrior, a poet and a musician, a deeply sincere believer and a romantic. He is credited with composing many of the Psalms - the intense religious poems in the Old Testament that are often set to music and sung in churches.

It was not to last. David disgraced himself when he fell in love with a married woman, Bathsheba, and arranged for her husband to die in battle so he could marry her. The Prophet Nathan condemned David for this and, although David repented, his rule was tainted by his selfishness. His family was split by plotting and betrayal, his two sons went to war over his kingdom and David died an unhappy old man.

David is a very attractive figure in the Old Testament. He has huge positive qualities but huge flaws. He is brave and reckless and imaginative; he has a great capacity for repentance when he does wrong and a genuine faith in God. However, he was a poor father, he could be selfish and destructive and he let power go to his head in the end. Nonetheless, he remains the best king Israel ever had and was looked back as an ideal warrior, ideal ruler and ideal believer.

David: king, lover, poet, musician...

The Davidic Royal Line

David left behind an united Israelite kingdom that was inherited (after a civil war) by his son **Solomon**. Solomon's rule continued Israel's 'Golden Age' and Solomon built the First Temple in Jerusalem to house the Ark of the Covenant and be the centre of the Jewish religion. Offered any gift he wished for by God, Solomon chose 'Wisdom' and God blessed him for this choice. However, like David, Solomon became corrupted by power and wealth. His death triggered another civil war and the kingdom split into two smaller states - **Judah** in the south, centred on Jerusalem, and **Israel** in the north, centred on Samaria.

The two Kingdoms continued as neighbours for 200 years. This was the time of the Divided Monarchy. In northern Israel, various families claimed the throne then lost it until, in 722 BCE, the Assyrian Empire invaded northern Israel and destroyed it as a state. Its scattered population became the 'ten lost tribes of Israel'. The survivors became the Samaritans who are mentioned in the New Testament and were viewed very negatively by the Jews.

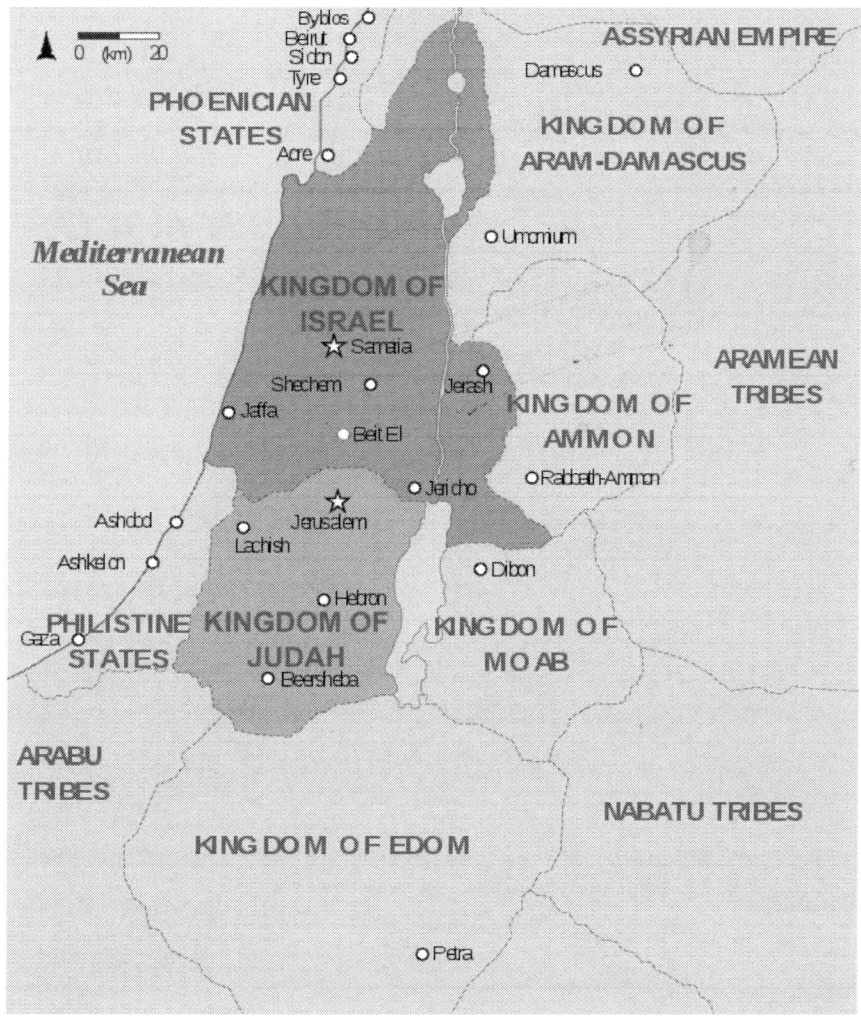

The southern kingdom of Judah was much more stable and was ruled for over 300 years by 'the House of David', a line of kings descended from David, making it one of the longest reigning dynasties in history. Although there's no direct evidence outside the Bible for David or Solomon, there is some archaeological evidence for the House of David.

The **Tel Dan Stele** is a carved stone with writing on it, set up by a local king to commemorate a victory in battle. It mentions Omri (the king of northern Israel) and an ally "*of the House of David*" ("BYTDWD") – i.e. a king of Judah. It dates from around 800 BCE.

Another carving is the **Moabite Stone** from 850 BCE which also seems to mention the House of David, although the text is damaged (it reads "BT--WD" with a missing portion in the middle but scholars think it read BT DWD, 'House of David').

These carvings tell us that the royal family of Judah in the 9th century called themselves the 'House of David' because they believed David was their ancestor. It doesn't prove David actually existed - but it does make it more likely that he did.

However, even the House of David could not stand against the great empires that were rising around it. Judah outlasted the unlucky Kingdom of Israel in the north, but, in 597 BCE, the Babylonians laid siege to Jerusalem, destroyed the city and its Temple and took the citizens away as prisoners of war.

The last Davidic king was **Zedekiah** who had rebelled against the Babylonians. The last thing Zedekiah saw was his children being executed before the Babylonian king Nebuchadnezzar had him blinded and imprisoned. That was the end of the House of David.

Or was it? We shall see...

The "Son of David"

The Davidic royal line was not a great success. Even while it ruled Judah, it had many bad and weak kings and only a few good ones (Hezekiah and Josiah stand out). Even while the House of David existed, many were dissatisfied and longed for a *true* "Son of David" - somebody who *truly* embodied David's fine qualities - to come to the throne.

After the destruction of Judah, this hope intensified among the exiles in Babylon. They believed that the bloodline of David still existed - it had 'gone underground' but it was still there. When the Jews returned to Jerusalem and rebuilt their Temple in 516 BCE, no Davidic king reappeared to sit on the throne. The Jews were ruled by other dynasties, such as the Hasmoneans and after then the hated Herodians; however, many Jews felt that these new royal families were illegitimate. The *real* king of the Jews would be a descendant of David.

This wasn't just wishful thinking. The Old Testament reports that God makes a promise to David:

> *Your house and your kingdom will endure forever before me; your throne will be established forever* - **2 Samuel 7: 16**

How could Jews make sense of this promise? The House of David had been destroyed in 597 BCE - had God broken his word? You might see a link here to the **problem of evil**: if God is all-good he will want to keep his promise to David and if he is all-powerful he will be able to keep his promise - but it looks like he hasn't kept his promise....

The Jews believed the answer to this was in two parts. First, God's promise *seemed* to have been withdrawn because the Jewish people had been sinful. God had allowed their enemies to triumph over them to teach them a lesson.

Second, Jews came to believe the line of David *does* "*endure forever*" and a descendant - a 'Son of David' - *will* appear to claim the throne. This Son of David will be a Kingly Messiah. He'll be different from the previous kings of the House of David because his rule will be a success: he'll defeat the enemies of the Jews, make them independent again, and this time the rule of the House of David "*will be established forever*".

The Babylonian Exile, in which the Jewish people were taken from their homeland, left a lasting effect on their religion and their hopes

What was needed for the 'Son of David' to appear? Jews had differing answers to this:

- **Religious Purity:** Since the destruction of Judah and the House of David had been a punishment for sins, Jews needed to return to the pure worship of God. Only once they had done this would the Son of David appear. However, groups like the **Sadducees**, the **Pharisees** and the **Essenes** (p59) had different ideas of what 'religious purity' meant

- **Military Action:** The Jews needed to 'start the ball rolling' by resisting the Romans; once the rebellion was in full swing, the Son of David would appear to lead it. Obviously, this view was popular with the **Zealots** (p67).

Does the Messiah have to be from the line of King David?

YES	NO
Kind David was the original messiah - anointed by God to be the best king. God's promise to David that his line would "*endure forever*" has to be fulfilled. So there has to be a descendant of David who will return to save the Jews from their enemies - the **Messiah**.	It's not proven that 'King David' really existed in history. He might have been a legend like King Arthur in Britain. Even if he did exist, his line was destroyed by the Babylonians and various 'messiahs' who tried to lead the Jews to independence - like Simon Bar Kokhbar - failed horribly.
The House of David failed because the Jewish people were sinful and turned away from God. When they return to worshipping God again and living morally, the Messiah will restore their kingdom and the line of David will rule it again.	The Messiah is more than just a warlord who wins battles. He's someone who will defeat evil, as God predicts in **Genesis 3: 15**; he might be a prophet as God predicts in **Deuteronomy 18: 15**. He's a wise teacher who will change people's lives, not a king from a failed dynasty.

ISAIAH'S SUFFERING SERVANT

One of the main sources for prophecies about the **Messiah** (p8)is the Old Testament book of **Isaiah**. However, Isaiah contains some passages which describe someone who does not fit the typical picture of a messiah - the **Suffering Servant**.

Isaiah

Isaiah lived in the 8th century BCE. He was probably from the royal family of Judah (the **'House of David'**) and he lived through difficult times. The Assyrian Empire destroyed the northern Kingdom of Israel and dispersed its population. When Judah allied itself with the Egyptians, they were next to be threatened: Jerusalem was twice attacked by the Assyrian army but miraculously survived. The Jews believed that angels had protected their city from the fate that befell their northern neighbour.

Isaiah's career as a prophet begins in 742 BCE with a shattering **religious experience** in the Temple, Isaiah has a vision of God on his throne, praised by angels while smoke and noise fills the Temple. This is a **numinous experience** for Isaiah - he is gripped by a sense of his own sinfulness and unworthiness. In his vision, an angel brings a fiery coal to his lips to burn away his sin. He hears God saying to his angels "*Whom shall I send*?" and the now-purified Isaiah calls out "*Here I am! Send me!*"

Isaiah's mission is to deliver to the people of Judah a very unpleasant message: God has condemned them for their sinful ways, particularly for their greed and mistreatment of the poor. The Assyrian Empire rising against them is an instrument of God's anger: God is ***using*** the Assyrians to punish the Jews for their sins. Isaiah predicts military defeat, slavery and humiliation for the people of Judah (in effect, saying that what happened to northern Israel will happen to them too).

> *And Isaiah turns out to be right - although it's the Babylonians rather than the Assyrians who actually destroy Judah and send the Jews into exile and this happens about a hundred years after Isaiah's death.*

Isaiah is no friend to the Temple priesthood either. He claims that God is sick of their sacrifices of animals and wants them to lead moral lives instead!

> *According to tradition, Isaiah was a vegetarian! In 1st century Palestine, the Essenes had similar criticisms of the priesthood at Herod's temple and the sacrificing of animals there.*

Among all the gloom and doom, Isaiah offers visions of hope. He predicts the future **Messianic Age** when wars between empires will end and the Jews will be able to live in peace in their land, worshiping God properly and leading moral lives. Isaiah goes beyond just predicting happiness for the Jews: he describes a future world where ***no one*** will have to suffer, a sort of paradise on Earth.

Because of this, Isaiah's prophecies have always been particularly important for people trying to identify the Messiah: what would he be like, what would he do, how could you recognise him? Isaiah seems to hold the answers but his prophecies are like riddles and can be interpreted in many ways.

The Servant Songs

An unusual figure keeps appearing in Isaiah's prophecies. This is the 'Suffering Servant'. The Servant serves God with total selflessness and loyalty. He is given a mission by God to lead the nations of the world. However, the Servant is mocked, abused and attacked by the people God has sent him to help. He endures his sufferings without complaining, intervening on behalf of other people and bearing their sufferings for them. Finally, he is murdered. However, God returns the Servant to life and rewards the Servant in front of the whole world. The people who had mistreated the Servant are stunned and ashamed.

The 19th century German scholar **Bernard Duhm** noticed that the references to the Suffering Servant are grouped together in four places and that these passages are actually poems or songs. They are known as the four 'Servant Songs'.

THE FIRST SERVANT SONG: ISAIAH 42: 1-4

God chooses the Servant who will bring justice to earth. The Servant is a **Kingly Messiah** and a **Prophetic Messiah** who brings about God's will on Earth.

> *Here is my servant, whom I uphold, my chosen one in whom I delight*
> *I will put my Spirit on him, and he will bring justice to the nation* - **Isaiah 42: 1**

Compare this to the description of Jesus' baptism as described in the Synoptic Gospels e.g. ***Matthew 3: 13-17***. *Notice how God is pleased with/delights in Jesus and puts his spirit into him.*

THE SECOND SERVANT SONG: ISAIAH 49: 1-6

This Song is from the Servant's point of view. He describes how he was called by God to lead not just the Jews but all the nations. The Servant will not be a political or military ruler but "*a light to the Gentiles*" - a source of inspiration and a teacher.

> *I will also make you a light for the Gentiles, that my salvation may reach to the ends of the earth* - **Isaiah 49: 6**

Jesus gives his disciples the 'Great Commission' to convert the Gentiles and Paul echoes this passage from Isaiah to justify why he converts Gentiles (non-Jews) to Christianity.

THE THIRD SERVANT SONG: ISAIAH 50: 4-9

The Servant describes the abuse he will have to face, but he is confident in God's protection.

> *I offered my back to those who beat me, my cheeks to those who pulled out my beard;*
> *I did not hide my face from mocking and spitting* - **Isaiah 50: 6**

This seems to predict Jesus' famous teaching that his followers should "turn the other cheek"; it also anticipates Jesus' own abuse at the hands of the soldiers who arrest him

The soldiers torture then mock Jesus (Matthew 27: 27-31)

THE FOURTH SERVANT SONG: ISAIAH 52: 13-53:12

This is the "big one" and the one you will want to show some knowledge of in the exam. It's very famous and the language and phrases from it turn up in church rituals and prayers. There are several quotes here but you don't need to learn them all - but you should learn one or two quotes from Isaiah to support your discussion of the Suffering Servant.

This Song, which takes up all of **Isaiah 53**, probably has the biggest impact. It describes the Suffering Servant as a "*man of sorrows*":

> *He was despised and rejected by mankind, a man of suffering, and familiar with pain -* **Isaiah 53: 3**

The expression "man of sorrows" is commonly applied to Jesus by Christians

The Servant doesn't just suffer for himself - he takes upon himself ***other people's*** pain and suffering, but nobody appreciates it. Instead, people regard the Servant as a victim and an evil-doer.

Surely he took up our pain and bore our suffering,
yet we considered him punished by God, stricken by him, and afflicted - **Isaiah 53: 4**

Compare this to Christians' beliefs about Jesus' torture and execution. Elsewhere in the Bible, anyone who is hanged or crucified is considered to be cursed by God.

The Song describes the Servant being put to death, but his death is an ATONING DEATH that brings healing to others.

But he was pierced for our transgressions, he was crushed for our iniquities;
the punishment that brought us peace was on him, and by his wounds we are healed -
Isaiah 53: 5

The link to Christian beliefs here is pretty clear. Jesus was "pierced" by nails for the sake of mankind's "transgressions" (sins). Christians believe that Jesus' wounds bring healing from original sin.

The Servant is "*led like a lamb to the slaughter*" (an expression that has entered the English language) but is completely silent: "*he did not open his mouth*".

Christians regard Jesus as the "lamb of God who takes away the sins of the world". The Gospels present Jesus as silent in the face of his accusers.

After this miserable death, God will restore the Servant to life again. But his sufferings will have saved other people.

After he has suffered, he will see the light of life and be satisfied;
by his knowledge my righteous servant will justify many, and he will bear their iniquities -
Isaiah 53: 1

For Christians, this predicts Jesus' atoning death and Resurrection which removes mankind's sins.

347-420 CE

Christian vs Jewish Interpretations

For Christians, the Servant Songs predict the Messiah - Jesus Christ - but a very different sort of Messiah from the King or Priest or Prophet that were expected by other groups. They predict a Suffering Messiah who will die an atoning death then be resurrected. The specific details in Isaiah struck many Christians as uncanny in their resemblance to Jesus' sufferings and their belief about the meaning behind his death. **Saint Jerome** said that Isaiah "*described all of the mysteries of the church of Christ so vividly that you would assume he was not prophesying about the future, but rather was composing a history of past events*".

However, there are some problems with this. There's no evidence that Jews of the 1st century believed that the Messiah was going to be a Suffering Messiah or that **Isaiah 53** predicted the Messiah. The Gospels describe Jesus' Disciples stunned reaction when they learn that he's going to die: they would hardly be so surprised if they believed the Messiah was destined to suffer and die.

Modern Jews do *not* regard the Servant Songs as predicting Jesus - they don't accept that Jesus was the Messiah. For them, the Servant is symbolic of 'Israel' (the entire Jewish nation, not the country) itself. Earlier in Isaiah, God refers to Israel as his servant:

> But you, Israel, my servant, Jacob, whom I have chosen, you descendants of Abraham my friend - **Isaiah 41: 8**

It is Jews who are sent into the world to be a "*light to the Gentiles*" through their religion, but it is Jews who are mocked and abused and tortured and murdered. It is Jews who hope that their sufferings will be vindicated by God and believe that, in some way, the sufferings of their nation will teach a valuable lesson to the rest of the world.

Morna Hooker sums up this interpretation of the Servant as 'Israel' like this:

> Israel, who has been chosen by [God] as his servant, is to be restored from Exile and will manifest God's glory to all nations - **Morna Hooker**

In the past, Jews might have thought of various anti-Semitic persecutions in connection with the Servant Songs (culminating in the Holocaust in the 20th century). Many scholars think the section of Isaiah with the Servant Songs was written by somebody else a century or two after the real Isaiah: they call this author 'Second Isaiah'. If this is true, the sufferings might refer to the destruction of Judah and the Jewish exile in Babylon - with the Jews who were taken into Exile suffering on behalf of the Jews who were left behind in Palestine. When the Jews returned to Palestine in 538 BCE, 'Second Isaiah' described their hopes by writing the Servant Songs.

> Israel had been subjected to terrible humiliation, she was oppressed and afflicted, taken from her own country and led like a lamb to the slaughter: but now her sufferings are over, and she is to return; she will be exalted and know prosperity again - **Morna Hooker**

*This is a **preterist** interpretation of the Servant Songs - they refer to events going on at the time they were composed*

Jews have other interpretations of the Suffering Servant. For some he represents, not **all** the Jewish people, but the holiest and best, the 'faithful few'. If this is true then the text is saying that anyone who devoutly tries to serve God is bound to suffer in this world - that would apply to the Messiah but it would describe lots of other sincere and good religious people too.

Both of these interpretations (the Jewish nation or the faithful few) treat the Servant as a CORPORATE PERSONALITY: he is a single person who symbolizes the experiences of a big group of people.

However, there are other ancient rabbis (Jewish teachers) who believe the Servant does represent the Kingly Messiah. When the Messianic Age comes, the non-Jewish nations will be ashamed of the way they treated the Jewish people now that their faith in God is backed up

Is the Suffering Servant supposed to be the Messiah?

YES	NO
The Servant is identified as the Messiah by several ancient rabbis who believed the Kingly Messiah would suffer. Isaiah links the Servant to the **line of King David**, just like a Kingly Messiah. The Fourth Song ends with God rewarding the Servant and bringing in the Messianic Age.	The Servant is a corporate personality, representing the whole Jewish nation (called 'Israel') or perhaps just the faithful few among the Jewish people who truly serve God. The Songs describe the sufferings of Jews at the hands of Gentiles (antisemitism).
The sufferings of the Servant closely fit the sufferings of Jesus, who was rejected by his own people, abused and tortured then painfully executed. This supports the Christian belief that the Servant predicts Jesus and that Jesus' death was an atoning death for the sins of mankind.	Although some later rabbis link the Suffering Servant to the Messiah, there's no evidence that Jews of the 1st century thought **Isaiah 53** described a Suffering Messiah. The link between the Messiah and the Suffering Servant was made by Christians **after** Jesus' crucifixion.

THE MESSIANIC SECRET

In 1901 the German scholar **Wilhem Wrede** published a controversial idea based on his study of the **Gospel of Mark**. Wrede proposed that Jesus had never claimed to be the Messiah and that his disciples didn't believe he was the Messiah. Only later, following the Resurrection, did Christians start to think Jesus to be the Messiah.

The Gospel of Mark

Mark is the second Gospel in the New Testament, coming after **Matthew**. Most scholars today regard it as the earliest Gospel to be written (the **theory of Markan Priority** is in **Topic 3**), being composed around 65 CE, 30 years after the Crucifixion. It is the shortest Gospel.

It begins with Jesus' baptism by John and features many stories of Jesus casting out demons and evil spirits as well as healing people. It ends with the Crucifixion and the women coming to Jesus' tomb on Sunday to find it empty. The earliest versions of Mark's Gospel end there, at **Mark 16: 8**. Later versions of the Gospel have descriptions of the Resurrected Jesus appearing to his Disciples,

There are some distinctive features of Mark's Gospel. Jesus frequently makes people promise to keep his identity secret when they realise he is the Messiah or when he performs miracles. Here are two examples:

- When Jesus asks his disciples who they think he is, Peter answers, "*You are the Messiah*" and Jesus commands him to keep this a secret

- When Jesus heals a leper, he tells the man not to tell anyone about this miracle (but the man disobeys and tells everyone)

Another feature is that Jesus reveals that he is the Messiah in **Parables** which his disciples cannot understand. For example, the **Parable of the Sower** seems to mean that Jesus is the Messiah and his teachings are a "*seed*" that will grow in some people's souls but not in others. Why doesn't Jesus say this more plainly? Jesus explains:

> *The secret of the kingdom of God has been given to you. But to those on the outside everything is said in parables* - **Mark 4: 11**

Wrede thinks that this means Jesus is ***deliberately*** being mysterious and speaking in Parables because he doesn't ***want*** ordinary people to know he is the Messiah

> *But why would Jesus not want people to know he was the Messiah?*

The Messianic Secret

Wrede has an explanation for the "Messianic Secret": **Jesus never claimed to be the Messiah.** However the later Christians of the 60s and 70s CE definitely *did* think Jesus was the Messiah. Wrede argues that this leads to

> *a tension in the belief of the Early Church of Jesus as Messiah and the unmessianic character of Jesus' ministry* - **MORNA HOOKER**

The argument goes like this:

- Jesus had an "*unmessianic ministry*" - he didn't set himself up as a King or a Prophet, didn't try to free the Jews from Roman rule; instead he taught a message of God's love and forgiveness and he died a very un-messianic death on the Cross

- Later Christians believed Jesus had been resurrected and that he WAS the Messiah. This meant that the Christians had very different beliefs about Jesus from Jesus' own friends and family and ordinary followers

- When Mark's Gospel was written, those followers and family were still around; they objected to Christians calling Jesus the Messiah because they remembered what Jesus had been like and they knew he had never made this claim for himself

- So Mark and the Christians like him replied that Jesus *had* claimed to be the Messiah but he had done so *secretly* - swearing the people 'in the know' to silence or speaking in Parables that only his 'inner circle' understood

Wrede concludes that the passages in Mark's Gospel where Jesus admits to being the Messiah are fictions. They didn't really happen. Mark invented them and then, when critics pointed out that such things never happened, Mark added the fictional detail that Jesus made everybody keep it secret.

This theory is based on **Markan Priority**. Matthew and Luke, because they were written later than Mark (probably in the 80s or 90s CE), didn't have to keep Jesus' identity a secret since, by that time, the original audience who remembered Jesus' ministry had all died off. Matthew and Luke repeat many of the same stories that are in Mark, but the theme of secrecy is much less important. They include other stories where Jesus is quite outspoken about being the Messiah (but if Wrede's theory is correct, these stories must be fictions too).

This theory ties in with the debate about the **Suffering Servant** (p17) being the Messiah. If 1st century Jews did not expect the Messiah to be a Suffering Servant, then that explains why they didn't think Jesus was the Messiah during his lifetime or immediately after his death. It was the Resurrection that made Jesus' followers think he was the Messiah, so stories about Jesus being recognised as the Messiah before he died cannot be historically true.

Criticising Wrede's Theory

Wrede's theory was initially popular but has been challenged in several ways, notably by **Morna Hooker** (1991).

First, not everyone accepts Markan Priority; many Catholics (in particular) continue to believe Matthew to be the first Gospel. If Matthew is first and since it does not contain this 'secrecy' theme, then we can conclude the details about Jesus identifying himself as the Messiah were NOT added in later

Second, there are many good reasons within the story for Jesus to keep some things secret. After healing the leper Jesus is mobbed by crowds and has to stop visiting the big towns. Being famous as a miracle-worker gets in the way of Jesus' real mission, which is spreading his message of love and forgiveness. Jesus doesn't ***want*** to be a celebrity so he keeps his miracles secret.

> *if he believed himself to be in any sense the Messiah, the last thing he would do was to claim the title for himself* - **Morna Hooker**

Third, people will misunderstand what Jesus means if they hear that he is the Messiah. They will expect him to raise and army or declare himself king. The authorities (who are already hostile) will silence him if they hear he is leading some sort of revolution.

> *it would have been misunderstood as a claim to political kingship* - **Morna Hooker**

Therefore Jesus distances himself from the idea of the 'Messiah' and uses the term **"Son of Man"** to describe himself (see **Topic 2** for a discussion of this term).

Jesus' remark about Parables could be interpreted differently. Jesus might not be saying that he doesn't want ordinary people to understand him. He might be saying that, as a simple matter of fact, some people 'can't handle' the truth about him but others can. He speaks in Parables so that those who are spiritually open to his message will understand but people who are close-minded will not be angered by hearing things they can't accept.

> *the truth about Jesus is at once hidden from view and yet spelt out on every page of the gospel'* - **Morna Hooker**

Finally, there's the Triumphal Entry where Jesus arrives in Jerusalem and is greeted as a king. This scene is described in **Mark 11: 1-11** and in the other Synoptic Gospels and in John.

Jesus makes no attempt to silence the crowd, who wave palms (symbolising liberation from oppression) and declare that he is from **the line of David** (p12). Jesus has obviously planned his entrance, arriving on a donkey to symbolise that he is coming in peace not as a warrior - and fulfilling a prophecy from **Zechariah** in the Old Testament about the appearance of the Messiah. There's no secrecy here but a very public claim by Jesus to be the Messiah.

Does the Messianic Secret prove that Jesus never claimed to be the Messiah?

YES	NO
The Messianic Secret is a theory which explains why Jesus is so secretive in Mark's Gospel but this secretiveness disappears in the later Gospels. It makes sense of Jesus speaking in Parables that hide his real meaning.	The theory exaggerates the secretiveness in Mark's Gospel. The healed leper doesn't keep the miracle a secret and Jesus is mobbed by crowds. The Triumphal Entry into Jerusalem is a public statement of Messianic identity.
The theory is supported by the view that 1st century Jews did not expect a Suffering Messiah or **interpret Isaiah's Suffering Servant** as a Messiah. Jesus' disciples would not have understood him identifying as the Messiah so these passages must be later fictions.	Not everyone agrees that 1st century Jews didn't expect a Suffering Messiah. There are other plausible explanations for Jesus' secrecy, such as wanting to avoid political entanglements or celebrity that distracted from his mission and message.

THE MESSIAH IN THE NEW TESTAMENT

The New Testament presents a very different view of the Messiah from that found in most of the Old Testament but Matthew's Gospel goes out of its way to identify Jesus as the Messiah predicted in the Old Testament, especially in the story of Jesus' birth. He uses **'Proof-Texts'** which are references back to prophecies in the Old Testament to show that Jesus fulfils these prophecies in unexpected ways.

The Gospel of Matthew

Matthew is the first Gospel in the New Testament. For centuries, Christians believed it was the oldest ad original Gospel, with Mark being a sort of edited version and Luke being based on Matthew but with additions. However, most scholars today regard Mark as the earliest Gospel to be written (the **theory of Markan Priority**). Matthew was probably composed in the 80s or 90s CE, 20 years after Mark. Matthew begins with Jesus' birth in Bethlehem and features many stories which are linked to prophecies in the Old Testament, proving that Jesus is the Messiah.

There are some distinctive features of Matthew's Gospel. It is a very 'Jewish' Gospel, featuring a lot of detail about Jewish beliefs and a lot of references to the Old Testament. This is why Christians used to think it was the earliest Gospel (since Jesus and his first followers were Jews it would make sense that the first Christian writings would have a strong Jewish tone). The author of Matthew's Gospel (we don't know if he was really called 'Matthew') seems to have been a Jewish Christian struggling with his Jewish heritage and belonging to a church that had members who were both Jewish Christian and Gentile (non-Jewish) Christians. Jesus is referred to as the "*Son of David*" in the Gospel, which appeals to the Jewish Christians. The Jewish people are referred to as "*Israelites*" up until the Crucifixion; after that they are referred to as "*Jews*" because the *real* children of Israel are the Christians who have faith in Jesus, including the Gentile ones.

The Birth Narrative

Morna Hooker claims that each Gospel has a prologue that works as a "*key*" to "*unlock*" the main themes and teachings about Jesus. Matthew's Prologue is an extended Birth Narrative that describes the circumstances of Jesus' birth in Bethlehem and how his family ended up living in Nazareth in Galilee. Hooker calls Matthew's Prologue the "*prophetic key*" because it focuses on Jesus as the Messiah and 'second Moses' predicted by the Old Testament prophets.

Matthew's Genealogy of Jesus

> *The genealogy isn't part of the Anthology #1 extract, although the rest of the Birth Narrative is. This means you don't need to study the genealogy - but you might find it interesting.*

Matthew's Gospel begins with a **genealogy** (family tree) of Jesus, tracing his family back through the line of David, to King David himself then further back to Abraham (the father of the Jewish nation). **Morna Hooker** points out that that the word Matthew uses for "genealogy" is *Genesis*. So Matthew begins his Gospel with a new 'Genesis', just like the first book of the Old Testament.

The Genealogy in **Matthew 1: 1-17** demonstrates that Jesus is of the royal **line of King David** (p12) - and therefore qualifies to be the Messiah since he is the "*Son of David*".

The Patriarchs	The Kings	After the Exile
Abraham	Solomon, David's son	Jeconiah
Isaac	Rehoboam	Shealtiel
Jacob	Abijah	Zerubbabel
Judah	Asa	Abihud
Perez	Jehoshaphat	Eliakim
Hezron	Joram	Azor
Ram	Uzziah	Zadok
Amminadab	Jotham	Achim
Nahshon	Ahaz	Eliud
Salmon	Hezekiah	Eleazar
Boaz	Manasseh	Matthan
Obed	Amon	Jacob
Jesse	Josiah	Joseph
David, the King	*(The Exile in Babylon)*	**Jesus**

Matthew points out a structure in the family tree: 14 generations between Abraham and David who became king around 1000 BCE, then 14 generations of Davidic kings until the Exile in Babylon in 597 BCE, then 14 more generations bringing us up to the birth of Jesus.

This 3 x 14 pattern suggests that Jesus brings history to an end: a process that began with God promising Abraham that his children were the Chosen People reached its low point with the destruction of the Davidic monarchy but is now complete with the birth of the Messiah. God once promised Abraham that "*all peoples on earth will be blessed through you*" (**Genesis 12: 3**) and the birth of Jesus fulfills that promise.

Raymond E Brown points out that, by linking Jesus back to Abraham, Matthew addresses two audiences: a Jewish audience would be interested in Jesus' descent from King David but a Gentile (non-Jewish) audience would be more interested in Abraham, because God had promised a descendant of Abraham would bring a blessing to "*all peoples on earth*"- including the Gentiles. Jesus is therefore the promised Messiah for **both** groups.

Problems with Matthew's Genealogy

The genealogy doesn't match up with the description of the line of David in the Old Testament - several kings have been missed out. Since this ruins Matthew's 3 x 14 pattern, **Raymond E Brown** suggests that Matthew probably didn't notice this; he must have taken this section of the genealogy from another book which already had those mistakes in it (in fairness, these kings' names sound very similar in Greek).

Similarly, there aren't actually 14 generations in each. How Matthew got to be so bad at arithmetic is a bit of a puzzle but a bigger problem is that Luke's Gospel offers another genealogy with *different names in it*.

Perhaps the biggest criticism is that, according to Matthew's own birth-narrative, Jesus isn't descended from these people anyway! He was born of a virgin, with no human father, so Joseph's descent from the line of David is irrelevant. The only human family Jesus is descended from is Mary's!

There are two main solutions to this:

1. Ancient scholars supposed that various adoptions and re-marriages had occurred, with Matthew recording the biological line and Luke the legal one. Others proposed that Luke recorded Mary's family tree. The problem with this view is that ancient Jewish law had no particular word for "step-father" and no concept of tracing the family line through the mother, so these theories cannot be backed up with evidence.

2. **Raymond E Brown** suggests that no Ancient Genealogy tries to be a precise historical document or a biological record. Ancient peoples created genealogies to make political or religious points, not to record the messy business of who had a child with whom - this was an age before marriage or birth certificates or DNA testing. Matthew's Genealogy is a religious claim: that the promises God made about a descendant of Abraham bringing a blessing to all the world and the line of David producing the Messiah had been fulfilled in Jesus.

> *Conservative Christians believe that the genealogies in Matthew and Luke describe actual histories and regard Matthew as Joseph's family tree and Luke as Mary's family tree.*

The objection that Jesus wasn't biologically related to Joseph anyway isn't as important as it seems. Adoption was common in the Ancient World and adopted sons (who were chosen) sometimes were held in higher esteem than biological sons. Legally and politically, an adopted child could be just as much an heir of King David as someone with a biological link back to the Davidic line.

Matthew's Birth Narrative & Proof-Texts

These passages form Anthology extract #1, so you need to be familiar with them all in a general sort of way and you should be able to analyse one or two parts in depth

Joseph Accepts Jesus as His Son

[18] This is how the birth of Jesus the Messiah came about: His mother Mary was pledged to be married to Joseph, but before they came together, she was found to be pregnant through the Holy Spirit.

[19] Because Joseph her husband was faithful to the law, and yet did not want to expose her to public disgrace, he had in mind to divorce her quietly. [20]

But after he had considered this, an angel of the Lord appeared to him in a dream and said, "Joseph son of David, do not be afraid to take Mary home as your wife, because what is conceived in her is from the Holy Spirit. [21] She will give birth to a son, and you are to give him the name Jesus because he will save his people from their sins."

[22] All this took place to fulfil what the Lord had said through the prophet: [23] "The virgin will conceive and give birth to a son, and they will call him Immanuel" (which means "God with us").

[24] When Joseph woke up, he did what the angel of the Lord had commanded him and took Mary home as his wife. [25] But he did not consummate their marriage until she gave birth to a son. And he gave him the name Jesus.

The Magi Visit the Messiah

[2] After Jesus was born in Bethlehem in Judea, during the time of King Herod, Magi from the east came to Jerusalem [2] and asked, "Where is the one who has been born king of the Jews? We saw his star when it rose and have come to worship him."

[3] When King Herod heard this he was disturbed, and all Jerusalem with him. [4] When he had called together all the people's chief priests and teachers of the law, he asked them where the Messiah was to be born. [5] "In Bethlehem in Judea," they replied, "for this is what the prophet has written:

[6] "'But you, Bethlehem, in the land of Judah, are by no means least among the rulers of Judah; for out of you will come a ruler who will shepherd my people Israel.'"

[7] Then Herod called the Magi secretly and found out from them the exact time the star had appeared. [8] He sent them to Bethlehem and said, "Go and search carefully for the child. As soon as you find him, report to me, so that I too may go and worship him."

[9] After they had heard the king, they went on their way, and the star they had seen when it rose went ahead of them until it stopped over the place where the child was. [10] When they saw the star, they were overjoyed. [11] On coming to the house, they saw the child with his mother Mary, and they bowed down and worshiped him. Then they opened their treasures and presented him with gifts of gold, frankincense and myrrh. [12] And having been warned in a dream not to go back to Herod, they returned to their country by another route.

The Escape to Egypt

[13] When they had gone, an angel of the Lord appeared to Joseph in a dream. "Get up," he said, "take the child and his mother and escape to Egypt. Stay there until I tell you, for Herod is going to search for the child to kill him."

[14] So he got up, took the child and his mother during the night and left for Egypt, [15] where he stayed until the death of Herod. And so was fulfilled what the Lord had said through the prophet: "Out of Egypt I called my son."

[16] When Herod realized that he had been outwitted by the Magi, he was furious, and he gave orders to kill all the boys in Bethlehem and its vicinity who were two years old and under, in accordance with the time he had learned from the Magi. [17] Then what was said through the prophet Jeremiah was fulfilled:

[18] "A voice is heard in Ramah, weeping and great mourning,
Rachel weeping for her children and refusing to be comforted, because they are no more."

The Return to Nazareth

[19] After Herod died, an angel of the Lord appeared in a dream to Joseph in Egypt [20] and said, "Get up, take the child and his mother and go to the land of Israel, for those who were trying to take the child's life are dead."

[21] So he got up, took the child and his mother and went to the land of Israel. [22] But when he heard that Archelaus was reigning in Judea in place of his father Herod, he was afraid to go there. Having been warned in a dream, he withdrew to the district of Galilee, [23] and he went and lived in a town called Nazareth. So was fulfilled what was said through the prophets, that he would be called a Nazarene.

THE VIRGIN BIRTH

Matthew describes the birth of Jesus from his father Joseph's perspective rather than Mary's (which is described in Luke). Joseph intends to divorce Mary when he learns she is pregnant but he has a **religious experience** - an angel visits him in a dream - which convinces him to adopt the child as his own.

Matthew makes his point by addressing Joseph as "*Joseph, Son of David*" - emphasizing the Joseph is of the line of David. He also connects the Virgin Birth back to a prophecy by **Isaiah**.

PROOF TEXT 1: ISAIAH 7: 14

> [22] All this took place to fulfil what the Lord had said through the prophet: [23] "The virgin will conceive and give birth to a son, and they will call him Immanuel" (which means "God with us").

This is the first of Matthew's **PROOF-TEXTS**. Proof-texts are references to the Old Testament that attempt to prove that Jesus is the Messiah.

> *Therefore the Lord himself will give you a sign: The virgin will conceive and give birth to a son, and will call him Immanuel* - **Isaiah 7: 14**

This is a much-debated passage. From a **preterist** interpretation, Isaiah is describing a royal birth back in the 8th century BCE - almost certainly Prince Hezekiah, son of King Ahaz. But what about the virgin conceiving? There are two explanations considered by **Raymond Brown**:

1. **The virgin conceiving might be a translation error.** Isaiah's prophecy is in Hebrew and uses the word "*almah*" to describe the mother: *almah* means "young woman" but not necessarily a virgin; Hebrew has another word, "*bethulah*", which means a virgin. However, when the Old Testament was translated into Greek, *almah* was translated as "*parthenos*", a Greek word which definitely means 'virgin'. Matthew used the Greek Old Testament and may have misunderstood what Isaiah had been saying.

2. **The virgin conceiving might not be intended to be supernatural.** After all, virgins conceive all the time. If King Ahaz's young bride was a virgin, then it would be natural to hope that, on her wedding night, she would conceive (losing her virginity in the process) and bear the king a son (and she did - the future King Hezekiah!).

> Both of these explanations assume that *Isaiah 7: 14* was never intended to describe a miracle. It was mistaken for a description of a miracle when it was taken out of its proper context (a royal wedding around 750 BCE) and translated into another language!

However, it's important to remember that *almah* **could** mean 'virgin' in this context and that the Jewish scholars who translated the Old Testament into Greek (200 years before Matthew wrote his Gospel) chose the Greek word *parthenos* so *almah* certainly meant 'virgin' to them! There's also nothing to stop **Isaiah 7: 14** being a DOUBLE-PROPHECY, something that refers to the (perfectly normal) birth of King Ahaz's son long ago and also, 750 years later, to the supernatural birth of Jesus Christ.

You'll notice that the prophecy speaks of a son being called 'Immanuel', (or 'Emannuel') not 'Jesus'. However, it's the MEANING of 'Immanuel' ("God With Us") that matters. **Morna Hooker** explains it like this:

> *The child who is about to be born WILL be known as 'Emmanuel', in the sense that in later days men and women will say that, through him, God was with them* - **Morna Hooker**

Isaiah's prophecy seems doubly-unlucky with names because, 750 years previously, King Ahaz didn't called prince Hezekiah 'Immanuel' either

THE VISIT OF THE MAGI

In tradition and Christmas carols, they are known as the 'Three Wise Men' or the 'Three Kings'. Tradition even gives them names: Caspar, Balthasar and Melchior. However, the Bible doesn't name them, doesn't number them to be three and they're not kings. They are *'magi'*, a word meaning a priest of the Persian religion specialising in astronomy and interpreting dreams. We get the modern words 'magic' and 'magician' from the ancient *magi*. The *magi* had a reputation in the Roman Empire for weird and exotic beliefs, occult powers and ancient wisdom (a bit like the druids over at the other end of the Empire in Britain).

Magi should be pronounced MAR-GEE but it people often say it as MAY-GUY or MAY-JYE. Why did readers assume there were three of them? Probably because their three gifts are named: gold, frankincense and myrrh.

The *magi* are not Jews - they are Gentiles. It is significant that the first people to recognise the Messiah are not Jews at all. Once again, this is Matthew indicating that God's promise to Abraham is being fulfilled: Abraham's descendant Jesus will be "*a blessing to all the nations*" rather than just to the Jews.

Matthew goes even further in this analysis. The Jews have the Old Testament Scriptures but refuse to understand what the prophets have said and refuse to worship the Messiah (instead, the King of the Jews plots to kill him); it is the Gentiles who understand the truth even though they didn't know the prophecies. This justifies Matthew's claim that the Christians - including the Gentile Christians - are the true followers of the Messiah.

The *magi*'s gifts are symbolic too:

- Gold is the gift for a king, representing Jesus as the Kingly Messiah

- Frankincense was burnt in temples during worship for its sweet smell; it represents Jesus as the Priestly Messiah

- Myrrh is a medicinal ointment with a bitter flavour; it represents Jesus' suffering and death as the Suffering Messiah or the Suffering Servant (a "*man of sorrows*")

Raymond E Brown points out some of the problems with this story. Why do the *magi* need to ask where the Messiah would be born, while in John 7: 42 everyone seems to know about the prophecy that the Messiah will be born in Bethlehem? Why doesn't Herod follow the *magi* on their 5-mile trip to Bethlehem? Why are there no records of the 'star' the *magi* followed, given that the Romans, Greeks and Persians did record a lot of astronomical events - and the Chinese recorded practically everything?

The last point might not be a big criticism. The 'star' might not have been a literal star; it might have been a conjunction of the planets Jupiter and Saturn passing over each other. We know this happened in 7 BCE and would have been incredibly meaningful to ancient astrologers like the *magi* who believed that great events on Earth were announced by the movements of the stars and planets. In fact, since the conjunction happened 3 times in 7 BCE, that would explain the star 'moving' in the sky.

PROOF TEXT 2: MICAH 5: 2-4

> [3] When King Herod heard this he was disturbed, and all Jerusalem with him. [4] When he had called together all the people's chief priests and teachers of the law, he asked them where the Messiah was to be born. [5] "In Bethlehem in Judea," they replied, "for this is what the prophet has written:
>
> [6] "'But you, Bethlehem, in the land of Judah, are by no means least among the rulers of Judah; for out of you will come a ruler who will shepherd my people Israel.'"

The next Proof-Text links Jesus' birth in Bethlehem to the Prophet **Micah**'s prediction that the Messiah would come from King David's home town of Bethlehem.

> *But you, Bethlehem Ephrathah, though you are small among the clans of Judah,*
> *out of you will come for me one who will be ruler over Israel,*
> *whose origins are from of old, from ancient times* - **Micah 5: 2**

Bethlehem had shrunk to a village in the 1st century, about 5 miles south of Jerusalem. It's interesting that Matthew describes Mary and Joseph living here in a house. There's no mention of a stable or a manger and there's no suggestion that Mary and Joseph are just visiting Bethlehem temporarily.

The first Christians had problems with Jesus' background - he was from Nazareth in Galilee, abut 80 miles to the north. Jesus' Galilean background was well known; he is often referred to as 'Jesus of Nazareth' or 'the Nazarene'. Galilee was a rather backward area of farmlands and fishing villages where the locals had a strong accent: they were regarded as bumpkins and yokels by the sophisticated people of Jerusalem. There are **no** prophecies about the Messiah coming from Galilee.

Matthew's solution is to propose that Jesus' family were really from Bethlehem all along; they moved to Nazareth later (as we shall see). Luke has a different solution: the family was from Galilee but was visiting Bethlehem at the time of Jesus' birth.

> *The story of Mary and Joseph arriving from Nazareth in Galilee because of a Roman census and finding nowhere to stay and putting their baby in a manger (presumably in a stable, although the bible doesn't say this), comes from Luke's Gospel. The two stories are often combined together (harmonized) but they are originally separate.*

Jesus' Galilean background passes what scholars call the **CRITERION OF EMBARRASSMENT**. In other words, it's a historical detail that was embarrassing for the early Christians because it counted **against** their beliefs that Jesus was the Messiah. They wouldn't make it up so it's probably historically true. Matthew's story about the family living in Bethlehem **might** be true, but it's also **exactly** the sort of thing Matthew would want to make up.

THE ESCAPE TO EGYPT

Joseph has another prophetic dream, warning him to leave Bethlehem and take his family to Egypt - only a 40 mile trip to get outside the territory controlled by King Herod.

The family stay in Egypt until the death of King Herod - which we know was in 4 BCE because Herod was a famous person who is described in many other ancient sources.

> *Although the BC/AD dating system is supposed to be based on the year of Jesus' birth, Jesus cannot have been born in 1 CE because that would be after the death of Herod. if Matthew's story is historically true, then Jesus must have been born around 7 or 6 BCE.*

PROOF-TEXT 3: HOSEA 11: 1

> [14] So he got up, took the child and his mother during the night and left for Egypt, [15] where he stayed until the death of Herod. And so was fulfilled what the Lord had said through the prophet: "Out of Egypt I called my son."

The escape of Mary, Joseph and Jesus into Egypt mirrors ancient history where Joseph (the son of Jacob/Israel) is taken to Egypt in **Genesis 37: 36**. In the Old Testament, the Twelve Tribes of Israel spend generations in Egypt, first as guests then later as slaves. This is known as the Sojourn. Eventually they are led to freedom by **Moses** - this is the **Exodus**.

Matthew connects this journey to a quote from the 8th century BCE prophet **Hosea** (a rough contemporary of Isaiah):

> *When Israel was a child, I loved him, and out of Egypt I called my son* - **Hosea 11: 1**

This prophecy clearly has a **preterist** interpretation. Hosea was writing about the Jewish nation and *'Israel'* is a CORPORATE PERSONALITY representing all Jews. Hosea is recalling the way God rescued 'Israel' from Egypt by sending Moses and he is promising that God will save the hard-pressed Kingdom of Judea from her enemies, the Assyrian Empire. The *'son'* Hosea is talking about is 'Israel' itself.

However, for Matthew, the *'Son'* is the 'Son of God', Jesus himself. This is pretty clearly not the meaning Hosea consciously intended, but it could be DOUBLE-PROPHECY, where the passage has a preterist meaning (events in the 8th century BCE) and a futurist meaning (predicting Jesus, 750 years later).

THE MASSACRE OF THE INNOCENTS

To protect his rule against a rival king who might grow up to threaten him, King Herod orders his soldiers to go to Bethlehem and kill all the boys under two years old.

Historically, there's no evidence for this massacre outside Matthew's Gospel. **Josephus Flavius** describes Herod's reign in his ***Antiquities of the Jews*** in 90 CE but never mentions this, although he describes how Herod murdered his own sons, wife and mother-in-law!

However, such a murder spree is quite in keeping with Herod's character. Since the population of Bethlehem at this time was about 1000, the massacre could only have involved about twenty children. **R.T. France** explains why the massacre isn't mentioned by historians, saying:

> *the murder of a few infants in a small village [is] not on a scale to match the more spectacular assassinations recorded by Josephus* - **R.T. France**

Raymond E. Brown argues that the story is supposed to echo the story of Moses, where Pharaoh of Egypt gives orders to kill the male children of the Hebrew slaves in **Exodus 1: 22**. Moses narrowly avoided being caught up in this mass-killing and Jesus is presented by Matthew as a "second Moses". Brown believes the story of the massacre is **symbolic**, not historical.

PROOF-TEXT 4: JEREMIAH 31: 15

> [16] When Herod realized that he had been outwitted by the Magi, he was furious, and he gave orders to kill all the boys in Bethlehem and its vicinity who were two years old and under, in accordance with the time he had learned from the Magi. [17] Then what was said through the prophet Jeremiah was fulfilled:
>
> [18] "A voice is heard in Ramah, weeping and great mourning, Rachel weeping for her children and refusing to be comforted, because they are no more."

Matthew links the massacre back to another Old Testament prophet, **Jeremiah**. Jeremiah describes the suffering of the Jews of Judah as they are taken away into Exile by the Babylonians in 597 BCE. The prisoners were assembled at a town near Jerusalem called Ramah before being deported. Jeremiah imagines the weeping of the mothers who will be separated fro their children. He compares this to a famous figure from the past, **Rachel** the wife of Jacob and mother of Joseph. Rachel died in childbirth near Bethlehem and is buried there. Dying, she wept that she would never see her sons again.

> *A voice is heard in Ramah, mourning and great weeping, Rachel weeping for her children and refusing to be comforted, because they are no more* - **Jeremiah 31: 15**

This prophecy has a preterist interpretation. 'Rachel' is a CORPORATE PERSONALITY: she represents all the women of the Jewish nation who are grieving throughout history. In this passage, 'Rachel' is weeping for the Jews in Exile in Babylon.

Rachel's tears are also tears of joy, because the midwife told her she had delivered a healthy boy. In Jeremiah's prophecy, the tears are also joyful because the Exiled Jews will return to their homeland (which they did, in 539 BCE).

Matthew takes a futurist interpretation, because for him 'Rachel' represents the mothers of Bethlehem weeping for their children, murdered by Herod. Matthew does not tell us that the tears are joyful, but we can interpret them this way because Jesus, the Messiah, has survived and, in the next passage, returns home from exile in Egypt. Like the previous Proof-Texts, this text is a DOUBLE-PROPHECY, describing events from 500 years ago but also (according to Matthew) predicting Jesus.

RELOCATION TO NAZARETH

King Herod dies in 4 BCE and Joseph, Mary and Jesus return home. However, Herod's successor is his son (two or three of them survived their father's rages) and **Herod Archelaus** is just as bloodthirsty as his father. Joseph is advised in a dream not to return to Judea at all, but to go to Nazareth in Galilee.

Bibles usually call this final journey the "return" to Nazareth - but Matthew has never suggested that Joseph and Mary came from Nazareth in the first place. It's Luke's Gospel that describes Joseph and Mary coming from Nazareth to Bethlehem for a census, staying there long enough for Jesus to be born, then going directly home to Nazareth again. For Matthew, Joseph is a citizen of Bethlehem. So why does he go to live in Nazareth?

Avoiding Archelaus would be a reason not to return to Judea. Archelaus certainly existed. He ruled until 6 CE. Sickened of his cruelty, the Jewish subjects complained to the Roman Emperor. Archelaus was deposed and sent into exile; his territory became the Roman province of Judea and a Roman governor was sent out to rule it directly. In the meantime, it makes sense that Joseph wouldn't put his family at risk by returning to a country ruled by Archelaus. However, Galilee was ruled over by King Herod's *other* son, **Herod Antipas**. Antipas wasn't quite as unhinged as Archelaus and he ruled Galilee right through Jesus' lifetime.

> *When the adult Jesus has run-ins with 'King Herod' - for example, the 'Herod' who executed John the Baptist - it is Herod Antipas the Bible is referring to.*

So why avoid returning to one country ruled by an evil son of the king who tried to kill your family, only to go and live in the country ruled by his brother? Why not live in neighbouring Decapolis instead?

Mathew has a religious reason to locate Jesus in Galilee rather than Judea. Judea is thoroughly Jewish but Galilee is a region of Gentiles where Jewish farmers and fishermen work alongside Romans and Greeks and Syrians and lots of other ethnicities. Matthew calls it *"Galilee of the Gentiles"*, echoing Isaiah who uses the same phrase. This fits with Matthew's theme that Jesus has come as much for the Gentiles (non-Jews) as for the Jews themselves.

Secondly, the fact that Jesus was a Galilean was too well-known to be ignored by Matthew. Everyone knew Jesus as the preacher and miracle-worker *from Galilee*. This fact passes the CRITERION OF EMBARRASSMENT because it's a biographical detail that Matthew and the other early Christians would probably have ignored if they could.

Joseph, Mary & Joseph's travels in Matthew's Gospel

There are no prophecies about the Messiah coming from Galilee, which is why Matthew has to explain that Jesus was *really* from Bethlehem originally and only *seemed* to be from Galilee.

PROOF-TEXT 5: ISAIAH 11:1

Despite the lack of prophecies linking the Messiah to Galilee, Matthew does make the link in his final Proof-Text.

> [21] So he got up, took the child and his mother and went to the land of Israel. [22] But when he heard that Archelaus was reigning in Judea in place of his father Herod, he was afraid to go there. Having been warned in a dream, he withdrew to the district of Galilee, [23] and he went and lived in a town called Nazareth. So was fulfilled what was said through the prophets, that he would be called a Nazarene.

A 'Nazarene' is somebody from Nazareth... but the Old Testament prophets never said that the Messiah would come from Nazareth or anywhere else in Galilee. What is Matthew talking about?

Raymond E. Brown suggests two possibilities. The first is a word-play. 'Nazarene' sounds like the Hebrew word **NE-TZER** which means "branch". There is a link here back to **Isaiah** who claimed that the Messiah would be of the **line of David** (p12), descended from David's father Jesse:

> *A shoot will come up from the stump of Jesse; from his roots a Branch will bear fruit -*
> **Isaiah 11: 1**

> *This sounds a bit strained but the prophecy about the messiah being a 'branch' of the Davidic family tree was very famous and so referring to Jesus as ne-tzer ('the branch') might have been recognised by Jewish readers as referring to the prophecy*

The second is that there was an old Jewish sect called the **Nazirites** that included great Old Testament heroes like Samson. The Nazirites were promised to the service of God while still in their mother's wombs, so this reference reinforces the theme that Jesus was born to be the Messiah. Samson was a flawed Nazirite but the TRUE Nazirite - the one who fully dedicates himself to God and does God's work on Earth - is Jesus.

EVALUATING MATTHEW'S BIRTH NARRATIVE & PROOF-TEXTS

On the face of it, Matthew's Birth Narrative seems to be on solid historical ground. There are geographically factual places (Bethlehem, Egypt, Galilee) and people (Herod, the *magi* of Persia, Archelaus). Compared to Luke's rather more fantastical Birth Narrative, there's just one miracle (the Virgin Birth) and the only angels that appear do so in dreams. The Virgin Birth might be a mistake based on Matthew misunderstanding **Isaiah 7: 14** and the only other improbable event (the Massacre of the Innocents) is not nearly so improbable once you understand the sort of atrocities King Herod certainly did carry out.

On further investigation, the Birth Narrative looks less plausible. It contradicts Luke's Birth Narrative (no Census, Joseph and his family go to Egypt rather than to Nazareth). More than that, there are wider inconsistencies. Matthew presents the birth of the Messiah as a political event attended by foreign dignitaries and triggering a mass-killing; Jesus' family become political refugees in another country. Yet these events are never mentioned by Luke or the other Gospelists. In **John 7: 42**, people say that Jesus can't be the Messiah because he's from Galilee.

> *Why didn't Jesus just point out that actually, he WAS from Bethlehem originally? Had no one heard of the Messiah being born 30 years previously and those poor children who were massacred?*

The Proof-Texts have similar problems. At first glance they read like striking predictions of Jesus' early life. On close examination, they are quoted out-of-context and describe events going on in the ancient kingdom of Judah, 750-500 years previously.

There are ways round these problems. Conservative Christians HARMONISE the Birth Narratives in Matthew and Luke, explain away the inconsistencies in the Genealogies and interpret the Proof-Texts as DUAL PROPHECIES that have both a preterist meaning (that the prophet consciously intended) and a futurist meaning (that the prophet perhaps did not intend). They can succeed in this, but the immediate simplicity and persuasiveness of Matthew's 'proof' is lost.

Scholars like **Raymond E. Brown** suggest that the Birth-Narrative should not be regarded as historical and wasn't even intended to be. Instead it is religious **symbolism** conveying Matthew's beliefs about Jesus being the Messiah, the 'new Moses' and the Son of David. It is written to reassure Gentile Christians that the Messiah is important to them too and to answer Jewish criticisms that Jesus did not qualify as being the true Messiah. Brown calls the Birth Narrative *"an attractive drama that catches the imagination"* but concludes that it is probably a PIOUS FICTION.

Morna Hooker regards the Birth-Narrative as a *"key"* that *"unlocks"* the rest of the Gospel, saying, *"the beginning of the story hints at the ideas that will be made plain at the end"*. It tells readers to look for similarities between Jesus and Moses as well as Jesus and King David (in other words, a Prophetic *and* a Kingly Messiah). It hints that the Gentiles will become Jesus' followers but the Jews will reject him. It warns readers that the evil rulers of this world will try to kill Jesus (and later his followers), but promises that their plans will fail because of God's guiding power.

Do the Birth-Narrative and proof-texts in Matthew prove Jesus to be the Messiah?

YES	NO
Matthew shows that Jesus was born in Bethlehem to a family descended from King David, exactly what you'd expect from the Messiah. He only moved to Nazareth in Galilee later and all along the way the key events of his childhood match prophecies from the Old Testament.	Matthew's Genealogy is very flawed and may well be fictional. The Birth-Narrative contains details (like the visit of the *magi*) which are very improbable or (like Herod's massacre of the innocents) are not recorded in independent sources from the time.
The Proof-Texts establish Jesus' Messiah-ship, such as Isaiah's prophecy that he would be conceived by a virgin or Hosea's prophecy that he would be called out of Egypt.	The Old Testament prophecies have preterist interpretations that are much more obvious and plausible, such as Isaiah celebrating the birth of Prince Hezekiah to a young bride or Hosea warning about the attacking Assyrians.

UNIT 1.2 THE WORLD OF THE FIRST CENTURY

The 1st century CE was a turbulent time in the region known as Palestine, covering the Roman Province of Judea and the neighbouring territory of Galilee. The Jews of this region faced challenges from the wider **Hellenic** (Greek) culture of the Mediterranean world that were both religious and political. They lived under the oppression of the **Roman Empire** and were forced to redefine their religion as a response. Because of this, they divided into many different groups.

> *Note: names can be controversial. The Edexcel specification refers to the region inhabited by the Jews in the 1st century CE as 'Palestine'. This is not a name 1st century Jews themselves used. Rather, it's the Greek/Roman term for the region. Today, the name has political connotations that did not exist in the 1st century.*

Life in 1st Century Palestine

Geography

The region the Romans called Palestine is in the Eastern Mediterranean, covering what today is the State of Israel and parts of Lebanon, Syria and Jordan. It is a land of contrasts: rugged mountains which see snow in the winter and scorching deserts that rarely see rain alongside lush farmland where grapes, dates and olives grow and sheep and goats are tended. In the 1st century there are villages of dirt huts built around precious wells, old towns of crumbling stone dating back centuries and new cities in the Greek style with marble columns and paved roads.

In the north is the Sea of Galilee, surrounded by fertile farmland and hills wooded with pine and oak. The Jezreel Valey connects Galilee to the coast. South of this rise the highlands of Samaria. A coastal plain stretches all the way to the Egyptian desert, and the valley of the River Jordan slices through the mountains until it flows into the Dead Sea, a lake so salty the plants and animals cannot survive in it (but King Herod made it into a health resort!). The mountains south of Samaria form Judea itself, dominated by the city of Jerusalem. The steep valleys are fertile but south and west of here the land gives way to the Judean Desert.

History & Politics

The southern part of Palestine had been the Jewish kingdom of Judah, until it was destroyed by the Babylonians in 597 BCE. When the Exiled Jews returned here in 539 BCE, they set about rebuilding their kingdom, conscious of God's promise in the Old Testament that the entire region was the 'Promised Land' given to the descendants of Abraham.

The Hasmonean family ruled Judea (as it became known) and managed to create a fully independent Jewish kingdom for about 50 years (from 110 BCE to 63 BCE) until **the Roman Empire** invaded the region.

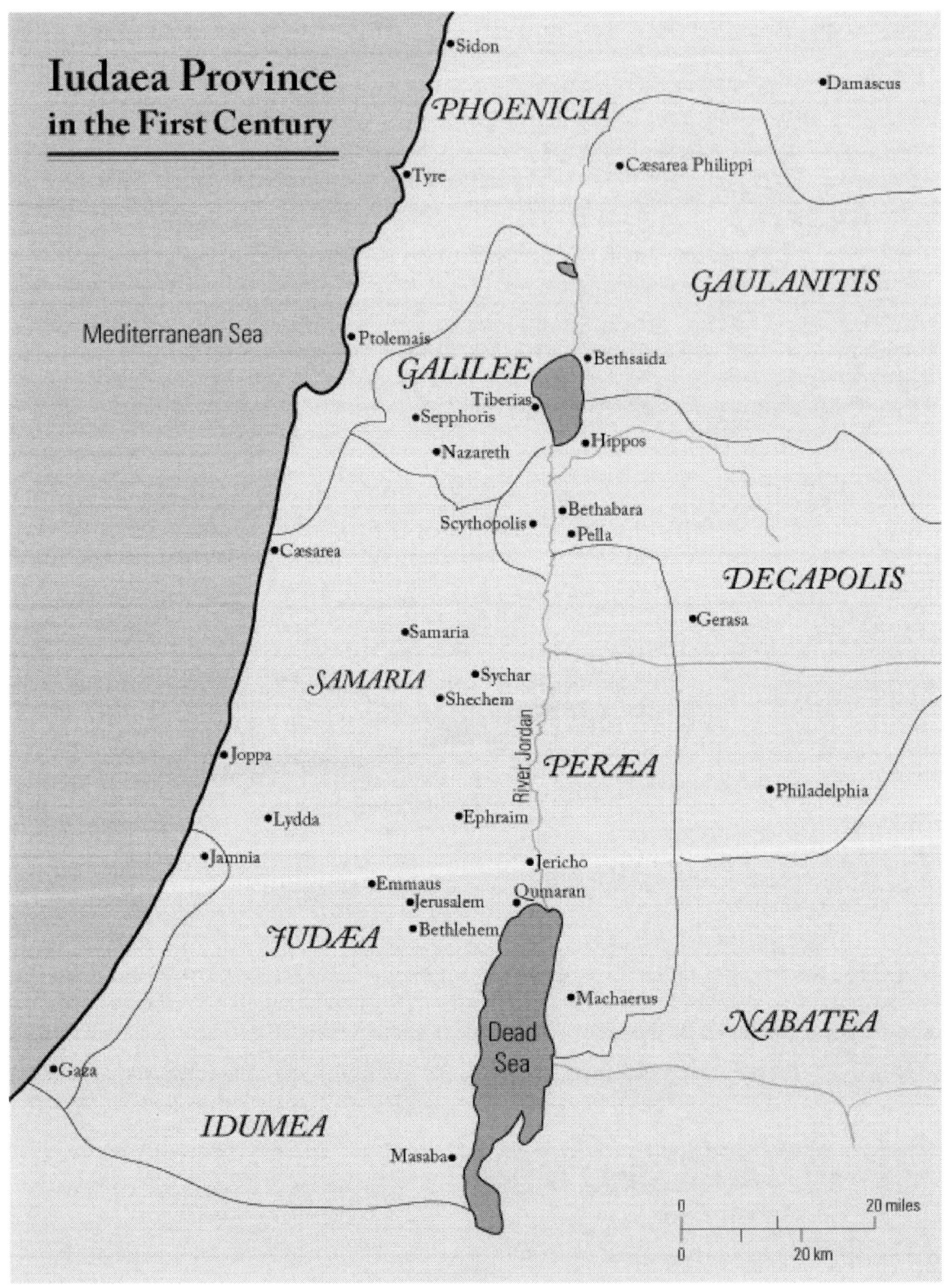

Iudaea Province
in the First Century

Mediterranean Sea

PHOENICIA

•Sidon

•Damascus

•Tyre

•Cæsarea Philippi

GAULANITIS

•Ptolemais

GALILEE

•Bethsaida

Tiberias

•Sepphoris

•Hippos

•Nazareth

•Bethabara

Scythopolis•

•Pella

•Cæsarea

DECAPOLIS

•Gerasa

•Samaria

SAMARIA

•Sychar

•Shechem

River Jordan

PERÆA

•Joppa

•Philadelphia

•Lydda

•Ephraim

•Jamnia

•Jericho

•Emmaus

Qumaran

•Jerusalem

JUDÆA

•Bethlehem

Dead Sea

•Machaerus

NABATEA

•Gaza

IDUMEA

Masaba•

0   20 miles

0   20 km

When the Hasmoneans rebelled against the Romans, they were crushed and in 37 BCE another family was installed as rulers who would be more loyal to Rome. These were the Herodians. **Herod the Great** ruled the region for 30 years, with the backing of the Roman Empire. He was unpopular with his Jewish subjects, because his family had only recently converted to Judaism and clearly did not take the religion seriously. Herod murdered many of his family members and oppressed his citizens: his death in 4 BCE came as a relief to the people. However, Herod left a legacy: the magnificent **Temple in Jerusalem** that he had expanded and lavished gold upon in a bid for popularity.

King Herod – terrible man but great builder

Herod's sons divided up the territory between them, but they were not as successful as their father. Herod Antipas ruled Galilee and had a scandalous personal life. Herod Archelaus ruled Judea with so much oppression and bloodshed that the Romans had him removed from power. Instead, they made Judea into a Roman province and sent a governor (a Prefect, later a Procurator) to run the territory for them. The governor's main jobs were to collect taxes and keep the peace. The governor was based in the coastal town of Caesarea but would travel 'up country' to Jerusalem for the annual festival of Passover, always a time when rebellions were likely. The Roman governor during Jesus' adult life was **Pontius Pilate**.

There weren't enough Romans to run Judea themselves: they needed helpers (or collaborators) to collect the taxes, report on troublemakers and impose the law. These people were known as PUBLICANS and were widely hated because they often demanded bribes and used their connections with the Romans to extort and bully their neighbours. Jews who became publicans were considered to have 'sold out'. Although Jewish publicans could get rich quick, they risked being ostracized by their community and some were kidnapped and murdered.

The Romans also relied on the Temple Priesthood to run the country on their behalf. The Temple Priests in Jerusalem employed their own soldiers and collected their own taxes and worked closely with the Herodian kings and the Roman governors. In the eyes of some Jews, this made them little better than publicans themselves.

The whole situation was deeply unstable - especially since the governor Pontius Pilate was an insensitive and brutal man. Eventually, things came to a head, 30 years after Jesus' lifetime, in the **Great Jewish Revolt** (66-73 CE).

The People

The main distinction in the people was between Jews and **GENTILES** (non-Jews). The Gentiles in Palestine included Greeks and Romans, neighbouring Egyptians, Syrians and Persians as well as people from the Decapolis (the 'Ten Cities'). It also included the Samaritans who considered themselves to be the descendants of the lost tribes of Israel but who were regarded as liars and heretics by the Jews of Judea. These peoples lived side by side, traded with each other and formed friendships. However, Jews who followed their religion strictly could not eat with their Gentile neighbours and certainly couldn't inter-marry with them.

The Gentiles had mixed feelings about the Jews. On the positive side, they respected the religion because it was known to be very old and 'old' meant 'good' in the Roman world. They admired Jewish social ethics, such as collecting money for charity and providing healthcare and education for the poor. However, they found some aspects of Jewish religion irritating, such as resting on the Sabbath every 7 days, the food laws and the way the Jews kept themselves separate. The Jews had a reputation for squabbling and fighting with one another and being difficult to govern.

Nonetheless, there was a lot of curiosity about Judaism. Gentiles would sometimes attend Jewish Synagogues and prayers. The *metuentes* were Gentiles who worshiped the one God of Judaism and imitated some Jewish practices, such as keeping the Sabbath and avoiding forbidden meats. A Jewish preacher like Jesus would have attracted audiences of Gentles as well as Jews.

It's difficult to know what the Jewish people of the 1st century looked like. The Old Testament Commandment forbidding images means that the Ancient Jews did not leave behind pictures of themselves. However, many stereotypes about their appearance are certainly wrong.

A lot of European art depicts Jesus and his disciples looking like white Europeans. This is probably wrong, but the other extreme in 20th century film is to make them look like Arabs, which is wrong too. Arab peoples existed but had not conquered the region of Palestine in the 1st century, but Greeks, Romans and Persians had, so it's likely that most of the population looked more like them. Greek and Roman rulers found it difficult to tell who was or wasn't a Jew by appearance alone.

The standard 'look' for men in the Mediterranean world of the 1st century was to keep hair cut short and to shave - no long beards. However, philosophers often defied fashion and stood out by growing beards.

Religious leaders and people who had taken religious vows may have let their hair and beards grow. The Jewish sect of the Nazirites refused to cut their hair or shave their beards - but we know Jesus wasn't a strict Nazirite because he drank wine.

The Arab head scarf (*keffiyah*) was NOT worn at this time in history, despite what you see in many films and illustrations. Women grew their hair long (usually with a centre parting) and covered their heads with shawls. However, they did not wear veils over their faces. The standard clothing was a tunic (knee length for men, ankle length for women) with a woollen mantle on top - or two mantles on cold evenings. The mantle was a sort of wrap-around cloak, like a toga. Religious Jews might wear a prayer shawl with tassels over their shoulders. People wore sandals in the dry summer or leather shoes in winter.

Towns & Cities

Most of the Jews in the 1st century were farmers or fishermen (especially in the Sea of Galilee). They lived in small villages and farms. However, these little communities existed alongside bigger towns built by the Greeks and Romans. For example, a couple of miles away from Nazareth was the city of Sepphoris with its mosaics and Roman theatres. Jews who moved to these exciting places could get rich and enjoy a much more sophisticated and luxurious lifestyle, but perhaps at the cost of their religious purity. Tiberias was considered such a decadent Roman city that strict Jews refused to live there.

Capernaum was a fishing village on the north shore of Lake Galilee where Jesus began his Ministry. He preached his first sermons and performed his first miracles there. It was the home of his first disciples: Peter, Andrew, James and John. The tax collector and publican Matthew lived there - tradition claims he is the author of Matthew's Gospel.

Archaeologists have discovered the Synagogue in Capernaum where Jesus would have preached

The Roman capital was on the coast: Caesarea had been built by Herod the Great and named in honour of Caesar Augustus, the first Roman Emperor. The Roman governor of Judea ran the province from here.

Deep in the country and high up in the mountains was Jerusalem, the ancient capital of King David. In the past, this had been a remote and rather small city. King Herod had enlarged this place too, rebuilding the Temple on a massive sale and turning Jerusalem into a **Hellenic** city that would be a wonder of the Roman Empire. Jerusalem's population of (perhaps) 50,000 tripled during religious festivals, with pilgrims flooding into the city along with Roman soldiers to police the streets. Jesus came here as a pilgrim for the Festival of Passover at the end of his life. Unfortunately, in 70 CE at the end of the Jewish Revolt, the Romans demolished the city completely and nothing of its grandeur survives in modern Jerusalem except fragments of ancient walls.

HELLENISM

Jews in 1st century Palestine experienced two powerful cultural forces. One was the Jewish religion expressed through the culture of the Old Testament, with its prophets, its Commandments and the festivals and traditions based upon it. The other was Hellenic civilisation, the international culture that had been brought into Judea by the conquering Greeks and the Roman Empire.

Understanding Hellenism

'Hellas' means Greece: 'Hellenic' refers to Greek culture and ideas and 'Hellenism' is the spread of those ideas into other societies. Greek ideas were spread by the conquests of Alexander the Great, which took his Greek armies through Palestine into Egypt, then all across Persia, through Afghanistan and into India. When Alexander died in 323 BCE, his vast empire was carved up by his generals who became kings over Persia, Egypt and Greece itself. One of these founded the Seleucid Kingdom which was based in modern Syria and held power over Palestine and most of the Middle East. The Jews of Palestine found themselves under the control of the Seleucids for 150 years.

The vast kingdoms left behind by Alexander caused mass migration and allowed communication across Asia and the Mediterranean. Distinctive Greek ideas about politics, art, philosophy and religion that had previously been limited to the small Greek city-states like Athens and Thebes were introduced to the wider world along with the Greek language. This language, called *koine* (it's pronounced KOY-NAY), became the international language of business and trade that would be learned by all merchants and diplomats.

> *The term for a second language that people learn for trade and diplomacy is LINGUA FRANCA (because French used to be this sort of language in Europe). Koine Greek was the lingua franca of the ancient world. The New Testament was written in Koine.*

The Impact of Hellenic Civilisation

Hellenic civilisation had a number of distinctive characteristics that were different from the Israelite civilisation the Jews had inherited from the world of the Old Testament. Many Jews resisted Hellenization (the spread of Hellenic culture by force) but others cheerfully embraced new fashions, ideas and pastimes as well as new religious beliefs.

Polytheism

Polytheism is the worship of many gods, rather than such one. The Greeks worshiped the Twelve Gods of Olympus (headed by Zeus) along with hundreds of minor gods, demi-gods, nymphs, monsters and heroes. This wasn't unusual - the Jews always had neighbours who were polytheists.

However, the Greek gods differed from the pagan gods of the Middle East in several ways. For one thing, they were very human: they had relationships with humans, took human form, visited Earth and had feuds and romances just like humans did. The myths and legends about the Greek gods were full of psychological symbolism and meaning that made them especially entertaining and thought-provoking. Greek-style religion was adopted by lots of other peoples across the Hellenic world who re-imagined their traditional gods and goddesses in the Greek style, often describing them as local versions of those Greek deities.

For the Jews, this sort of Hellenic religion was very threatening. Their God had no physical appearance: he couldn't be painted or described. The Jews reacted with horror to the appearance of statues of the Greek gods and demi-gods like Hercules in their towns and in their Temple. Back in 168 BCE, the Seleucid king Antiochus had imposed Hellenization by force: he invaded Jerusalem and set up a statue of Zeus in the Temple. This led to a revolt by led the Maccabee brothers and a civil war between Hellenized Jews and the traditionalist Jews. The Macabees won, reclaimed their Temple and founded the Hasmonean dynasty that ruled Judea for a hundred years.

The Maccabee Revolt was looked back on with great pride by many 1st century Jews, especially those who still opposed Hellenization. King Herod the Great was a keen Hellenizer who set up many pictures of Greek gods in Jerusalem (but not in the Temple itself - he learned THAT lesson) along with a theatre and a circus where wrestling tournaments took place.

Humanistic Art & Leisure

The Greeks had developed striking new art forms that helped spread Hellenic civilisation: theatre and sculpture were the main ones. Of course other civilisations had acting and carved statues (think of the Sphinx!) but the Greeks brought something new to this: Humanism, which is a delighted interest in the human situation and the human body. Greek sculpture explored the human body in realistic detail and idealised it - made nakedness into a thing of beauty.

Greek theatre focused on human relationships and human psychology. Greek tragedies explored freewill and what it means to be human; Greek comedies poked fun at sex, religion and politics.

Did Jesus ever visit the theatre in Sepphoris, just an hour's walk away from Nazareth?

Linked to the Hellenic arts were new forms of leisure. Theatre-going became popular but so did the gymnasium. The Greeks obsessed over sport, particularly athletics, and their athletes competed naked. Linked to the gymnasiums were bath houses where the men and women (separately, not together) socialised naked in steam rooms and swimming pools. The Romans carried on this interest in public bathing and public nakedness, inspired by the Hellenic idealisation of the human body.

For the Jews, this too was unacceptable. The Second Commandment forbids making "*graven images*" and Jewish culture strongly frowned on nudity. Gymnasiums and bath houses were shameful places for traditionalist Jews. Such believers would not allow their great prophets Moses or Abraham or King David to be played on stage by an actor, especially in a play that presented them as flawed and complex human beings (although, to be fair, the Old Testament itself presents them as flawed on occasions and so does the Jewish storytelling tradition).

Rational Philosophy

The Greeks also developed a powerful philosophical tradition - indeed they invented the *word* "philosophy". This philosophical tradition included the ideas of Socrates which were developed by Plato into a school of philosophy (the 'Academy'). Plato's ideas were taken in different directions by the Stoics and the Cynics who offered codes of living that didn't depend on religion. Plato's student Aristotle rejected Platonism completely and developed his own influential approach to science, ethics and metaphysics.

Stoicism became the unofficial 'religion' of the Roman Empire. Stoics believed in one God, but they were Deists who did not believe God intervened through miracles. Instead they believed everything was predetermined (no freewill) and practised emotional restraint and a strict honour code to make life meaningful. Stoicism recommended suicide as the moral course of action under certain circumstances.

Cynicism was a more unusual philosophy. Today, 'cynicism' means a nasty disbelief in goodness and morality. However, the Ancient Cynics believed that the best life was a life that followed nature rather than social expectations. They recommended giving up material possessions and turned away from society. Cynic philosophers could be very unconventional but people sought them out for advice.

My favourite Cynic anecdote is about Alexander the Great going to visit the famous Cynic philosopher Diogenes. He finds Diogenes sleeping in the sunshine. Diogenes wakes up when the conqueror of the world asks him, "What can I do for you?" The philosopher says, "You can get out of my sun!" and goes back to sleep! Alexander is so struck by the philosopher's total self-sufficiency he says to his courtiers, "If I wasn't Alexander, I would be Diogenes!"

The point about these philosophies was that they had been arrived at by rational thought, not religious revelation. This contrasted with the Jewish religion, which came from revelations given by God to Moses and the later prophets. To many Jews, the philosophical basis of their religion seemed weak.

Many of them applied the ideas of Aristotle to their Judaism, linking God to the Unmoved Mover in Aristotle's arguments. However, the Unmoved Mover of Aristotle was very different from the stormy, emotional, intervening God of the Old Testament. **Philo of Aexandria** (20 BCE - 50 CE) applied Greek thought to his Jewish faith. Philo treated the stories in the Old Testament as **allegories** (stories with symbolic meaning that weren't literally true) and applied Aristotle's concept of the **Logos** to Judaism (you will learn more about this in **Topic 2**).

Probably the biggest philosophical idea to affect Judaism was the belief in PERSONAL IMMORTALITY (life after death). The Old Testament barely mentions the Afterlife and most Jews did not believe in a Heaven after death: you had one life to worship God and that was it! Plato's ideas about people having immortal souls that live on after death proved very popular with some Jews.

Cultural Relativism

Perhaps the biggest impact of Hellenism was unintentional. Alexander's enormous empire opened people's horizons. It showed them that they lived in a vast and varied world and brought them into contact with ideas, customs and religions from all across Asia and the Mediterranean. One effect of this was to produce a sense that there's nothing special about your own culture and the customs and beliefs you were brought up with. Relativism suggests that no culture is 'best' and no religion is 'true'.

This view was summed up by the Greek philosopher **Xenophanes** around 500 BCE. Xenophanes pointed out that the Ethiopians in Africa think their gods have black skin and the Thracians in Europe think their gods have white skin. He adds that if cows, horses and lions had hands, they would draw their gods with their animal bodies too.

This was a troubling idea for many Jews. It suggested that their God was really no different from the other gods worshiped by other people: no different from Zeus in Greece or Ahura Mazda in Persia or Ra in Egypt. This would mean there was "nothing special" about Judaism.

The Relationship of Hellenism with Jesus' Life & Work

Jesus grew up in Galilee, a place where Hellenic ideas mixed with Jewish beliefs. Was Jesus a Hellenized Jew?

Clearly, Jesus believed in life after death and personal immortality. These ideas had been growing in importance in Judaism for several centuries but many traditionalist Jews (like the **Sadducees**, p62) still rejected the Afterlife. John's Gospel links Jesus to the **Logos (Word) of God**, which is a Hellenic concept and might have been an idea that Jesus taught to his followers.

Jesus also directs his followers to take his message to the Gentiles as well as the Jews. This 'Great Commission' is in keeping with a Hellenic (universal) outlook rather than a narrow purely-Jewish one.

> *Therefore go and make disciples of all nations, baptizing them in the name of the Father and of the Son and of the Holy Spirit* - **Matthew 28: 19**

> *Although Matthew puts these words into the mouth of the resurrected Christ, we cannot be sure who really said them. while alive, Jesus seemed to have the opposite view that his mission was solely to the Jews. The 'Great Commission' might reflect the beliefs and priorities of gentile Christians after Jesus' time.*

Some scholars go further than this. **John Dominic Crossan** argues that Jesus was in fact a Cynic philosopher. He points out that the **Q Source** is the oldest account of Jesus' teachings and seems to reflect a Cynic philosophy: give up material possessions, turn your back on the world, live a simple and humble existence. In further support of this, the town of Gadara, 8 miles north of Nazareth, was known to be a centre for Cynic philosophy. Crossan argues that Jesus' Cynic philosophy was ditched by his later followers who came to view him as the Suffering Messiah, which he had never claimed to be (a view shared by supporters of the theory of the **Messianic Secret**).

However, critics of Crossan point out that even in the earliest sources Jesus predicts **the coming Kingdom of God**, which is definitely not a Cynic idea. This puts Jesus more in the Prophetic tradition of the Old Testament than the Hellenic tradition of the Cynics. Moreover, Cynics usually behaved in shocking ways, encouraging nudity and sexual shamelessness, but Jesus didn't teach these things. On the contrary, Jesus taught quite a severe sexual ethic about marriage and chastity.

Does Jesus have to be understood in a Hellenic context?

YES	NO
Jesus taught a doctrine of life after death, which is a Hellenic concept not found in the Old Testament. The Sadducees opposed this teaching and believed that life ends at death. Jesus' 'Great Commission' shows that he intended his message for the wider Hellenic world, not just to the Jews.	Although not described in the Old Testament, personal immortality had been taught in Judaism for several centuries and was not viewed as a 'foreign' idea. The 'Great Commission' may tell us more about the Hellenic views of Jesus' Gentile followers than Jesus' own views.
Jesus is best understood as a wandering philosopher of a type that was common in the Hellenistic world, especially among the Cynic philosophers. His teachings about giving away wealth and leading a simple life trusting in God to provide are very similar to Cynic views.	Jesus also opposed certain Cynic views, because he preached about the coming Kingdom of God. Also, Cynics taught people not to be ashamed of nudity and sex, but Jesus taught a rather conservative sexual ethic that sex belonged in marriage.

ROMAN OCCUPATION

Jews in 1st century Palestine lived under foreign rule. The people of Judea were ruled directly by a Roman governor who dealt brutally with dissent; in Galilee and elsewhere, Herod Antipas was a client king who ruled because he was backed by Roman military might. Rebellions were always brewing in the provinces of the Empire because of heavy taxes and corrupt officials, but in Galilee and Judea the religious beliefs and Messianic hopes of the Jews produced a particularly dangerous atmosphere.

Judea in the Roman Empire

Understanding the Roman Empire

The Roman Republic flourished in the 1st Century BCE. The Republic was based in Rome in Italy and ruled by a Senate rather than a king (an unusual arrangement for the time) but it had achieved almost total control of Mediterranean trade and dominated the old Hellenistic Kingdoms of Greece and Asia. The Romans enthusiastically absorbed Hellenistic culture (which wasn't very far removed from their own Italian traditions): they identified their own Italian gods with Greek gods (so Jupiter was identified with Zeus, Mars with Ares, Venus with Aphrodite, etc); they adopted public bathing and athletics, theatre and philosophy; they took a relativistic view about religion, as illustrated by Seneca's quote.

> *For most of the people in the Empire, the divine emperor was just one more god to worship. However, the cult of the divine emperor posed a religious problem for Jews (and later for Christians) because their religion forbade them from worshiping any other god.*

When Julius Caesar was assassinated in 43 BCE, the Roman Republic fell into a civil war which engulfed the whole Mediterranean world for 15 years. Augustus Caesar became the first Emperor of the new Roman Empire, followed in 14 CE by his step-son Tiberius.

> *Augustus was emperor when Jesus was born and Tiberius was emperor when Jesus was crucified.*

The new Emperors took grand titles and Augustus declared himself to be the 'Son of God' (*Divi Filius*). Augustus made sure his statues (such as te one on the left) were placed in temples around the Empire where they were worshiped. Worshiping the Emperor was worshiping the Empire itself - and refusing to worship him was an act of rebellion as well as blasphemy.

The Empire allowed local kings to carry on ruling their populations, so long as they were loyal to the Emperor and paid taxes to Rome. One of these local kings was King Herod the Great, who wrangled his way through the whole Civil War and stayed in power under the new Emperor. Areas that were too important or too troublesome to be entrusted to some local king were ruled directly from Rome: a governor was sent out to rule the province with the Emperor's authority. This is what happened to Judea. In 26 CE, the new governor was Pontius Pilate, a man with a reputation for brutality and arrogance.

So long as taxes were paid and the peace was kept, the Romans largely left their client kingdoms and provinces alone. Some people were 'Roman Citizens' who had particular privileges: they could travel freely within the Empire and they could appeal to Roman law rather than be judged by local kings and magistrates. Citizens would be spared the most feared punishment dealt out to runaway slaves, outlaws and rebels: death by crucifixion, the victim impaled on a post and dying by slow suffocation in public (usually at the side of the road) as a warning to others. At first, all Roman Citizens were actual Italians, but gradually citizenship was given out to more and more people. The Empire didn't impose Latin on everyone: throughout most of the Mediterranean, KOINE Greek remained the *lingua franca* (language of travel and trade).

The Roman legions were the most efficient fighting force in the world at that time and in the 1st century CE they were at their peak. A local governor in a place like Judea couldn't command an elite legion. Instead, the governor would command a force of Auxiliaries: soldiers recruited locally. The governor of Judea employed Syrians and Samaritans to keep the peace in Judea. Just like real legionaries, these soldiers would have to worship the Divine Emperor (which is why no religious Jews ever signed up to serve in the army!). Rome couldn't run the Empire with just soldiers. A civilian 'army' of publicans managed the complicated tax system. These agents had a free hand to demand bribes or impose fines and skim off money for themselves, so long as the Emperor got paid his taxes.

The Impact of Roman Occupation

For many Jews in 1st century Palestine, Roman occupation was fairly distant from their daily lives. In Galilee, where Jesus grew up, the ruler was a client king, Herod Antipas, so many of the magistrates and soldiers would have been locals. However, it was well-known that Antipas was only a puppet for the Roman Emperor and the population resented him and his minions. They also resented the publicans who collected taxes; some publicans were Jews who had turned their backs on their own kind to work with the enemy. These Jews were ostracized by their neighbours, sometimes threatened and killed. Since they had no choice but to socialise with Gentiles (and since some of their fellow-Jews wanted to kill them), many abandoned their Jewish faith altogether.

In Judea, things were more complicated because a Roman governor, **Pontius Pilate**, ruled the province directly. The governor used great brutality to put to riots and protests; troublemakers were crucified along public roads as a lesson for everyone else. Jews had a particular dread of crucifixion because the victim of this punishment is considered cursed by God, according to the Old Testament.

Interacting with the Roman Empire was difficult for Jews because many significant business deals, legal hearings or political meetings would involve a pagan sacrifice (normally burning incense or offering water or milk) to the gods of the Empire or to the Divine Emperor himself. Jews could not do this without breaking the First Commandment (which forbids worshipping any other God).

However, Judaism was considered *religio licita* - a protected religion. This meant that Roman officials would go to certain lengths to 'work around' Jewish restrictions about making sacrifices, working on the Sabbath or dining with Gentiles. In return, twice each day, the Jewish priests in the Temple in Jerusalem sacrificed two lambs and an ox for the wellbeing of the Empire and the Emperor.

Despite this arrangement, both sides felt irritated and exploited. To the Romans, the Jews seemed unreasonable and troublesome; to the Jews, the Romans seemed to be insulting their faith at every turn.

The Roman governor (his rank was "Prefect") was **Pontius Pilate**. Pilate was an arrogant man who was very insensitive to the Jewish religion. One of his first acts was to bring banners with pagan symbols into Jerusalem, triggering a riot. Several 1st century writers (including **Flavius Josephus**) describe Pilate's temper and stubbornness. Pilate worked closely with the High Priest of the Temple in Jerusalem, Joseph Caiaphas. The High Priest was appointed by the Romans and was expected to keep the Judean population in line. At the annual festival of Passover every Spring, Jerusalem was so crowded with pilgrims that keeping the peace became difficult. Pilate would travel from his coastal base at Caesarea to stay in Jerusalem for 10 days and his soldiers would police the streets. This was a tense time, because any rebellion against the Roman Occupation was probably going to start during Passover.

The Relationship of Roman Occupation with Jesus' Life & Work

One of the main features of Roman occupation in Jesus' Ministry is the appearance of publicans. Jesus tells a **Parable of a Pharisee and a Publican** (Tax Collector), where he praises the humble faith of the publican and condemns the spiritual pride of the Pharisee (p63). It's hard to underestimate how shocking this contrast would be to Jesus' 1st century listeners.

Jesus didn't just praise the faith of publicans, he socialised with them. **Mark 2: 15-17** describes Jesus being criticised for dining with publicans and replying that these sinners need God's love and forgiveness more than ordinary Jews.

> *Did Jesus tell these publicans to give up working for the Romans? Presumably not, since he wouldn't have been criticised if that's what he did. We can assume his message was that God forgives sinners and that, though the publicans had ruined their relationship with their fellow-Jews, they had not been abandoned by God.*

Jesus made converts of publicans. The Gospels mention Zacchaeus, the chief publican of Jericho, but also Matthew, a tax-collector in Capernaum whom Jesus approached at his money-counting booth and said, "*Follow me!*" According to tradition, this is the very Matthew who wrote **Matthew's Gospel**.

Taxes have an important role in Jesus' life. When asked whether a good Jew should pay taxes to Rome, Jesus cleverly points to the image of Caesar on a coin and says:

give back to Caesar what is Caesar's, and to God what is God's - **Matthew 22: 21**

> *This seems to be saying, give the Roman Empire the coins it wants but give God the worship and moral living he wants. However, these words are turned around to trap Jesus after his arrest, when he is accused of opposing the paying of taxes to Rome.*

A coin with the Emperor Tiberius' image – Jesus might have held just such a coin

Roman soldiers also appear in the Gospels. In Capernaum, Jesus is asked by a 'Centurion' (army officer) to heal his servant. Jesus praises the faith of the Centurion and announces that Gentiles like this will be rewarded by God alongside Jews.

> *Truly I tell you, I have not found anyone in Israel with such great faith. I say to you that many will come from the east and the west, and will take their places at the feast with Abraham, Isaac and Jacob in the kingdom of heaven* - **Matthew 8: 10-11**

The appearance of publicans and Roman soldiers emphasises the theme in the Gospels that Christ's mission is as much to the Gentiles as to the Jews. Matthew's Gospel often has scenes where Gentiles recognise Jesus' authority as the Messiah but Jews do not.

Of course, the main role the Romans play in Jesus' story is at his execution. Jesus is arrested by the High Priest, but handed over to the governor, Pontius Pilate, to be put to death. Under Roman law, the Jewish authorities could not execute criminals: only the Emperor's official could pass the death sentence on a criminal. All four Gospels present Pilate as strangely unwilling to execute Jesus. However, Pilate asks Jesus an important question:

> *the governor asked him, "Are you the king of the Jews?" "You have said so," Jesus* replied - **Matthew 27: 11**

> *Jesus' reply isn't a weasel-worded attempt to get out of answering: it's the humble way of agreeing, rather like saying "yes indeed!" or "quite so!"*

Luke's Gospel is even more explicit about the accusations leveled against Jesus by the High Priest and his mob:

> *"We have found this man subverting our nation. He opposes payment of taxes to Caesar and claims to be Messiah, a king."* - **Luke 23: 2**

Although Pilate can't have cared much about (or even understood) the title 'Messiah', claiming to be the 'King of the Jews' is a rebellion against Roman rule in Judea. 'King of the Jews' was a title given to Herod the Great by the Emperor: only the Emperor decides who is 'King of the Jews'. Opposing paying taxes to the Roman Empire is very serious. Pilate's main job was to ensure that Rome received its taxes. These crimes amount to SEDITION (trying to overthrow the government) and the Roman punishment for that was crucifixion.

Does the Roman occupation of Palestine make a difference to our understanding of Jesus?

YES	NO
Jesus' Ministry was shaped by the context of occupation: there were two people claiming to be 'Son of God' in the 1st century - Jesus and the Roman Emperor. Jesus' values of love and forgiveness contrast with the violence and brutality of Roman rule. Jesus was executed by the Romans because the values he represented threatened their regime.	Jesus' Ministry is shaped by the Prophetic tradition of the Old Testament, where King David is often referred to as 'Son of God'. Jesus' values are more in contrast with the harsh laws of the Old Testament. Jesus was arrested and sentenced to death by the Jewish priests - and Jesus recognises that the Jews persecute their own prophets without help from the Romans.
Without understanding the Roman occupation, the role of publicans makes no sense. The central question for 1st century Jews was how were they to practise their religion in a world where temporal power rests with an irresistible pagan Empire. Jesus offers an answer to that question that is still relevant for Christians today in a world of unbelievers.	Jesus' teachings about love and mercy and his Parables have lasted down the centuries and still speak to people today. Since Jesus was sent to die an Atoning Death it doesn't matter which regime killed him or which form of execution they used. It would have happened even if Judea was ruled instead by the Persians or by one of Herod's sons.

RELIGIOUS GROUPS IN PALESTINE

A century of rule by foreigners and misrule by Jewish kings who were not of the line of David had left the Jews of 1st century Palestine politically divided. The impact of **Hellenism** (p47) divided them still further. Should they embrace these new beliefs and lifestyles or reject them - and if they rejected them, how should they live as an alternative?

*Most of what we know about these groups comes from a writer called **Flavius Josephus**. Josephus was a Jew who fought in the Jewish Revolt, but after being defeated he changed sides to work for the Romans. His book **Antiquities of the Jews** (c. 95 CE) describes the Sadducees, Pharisees and Essenes as well as the (unnamed) Zealots. Josephus is a fascinating person; it's a shame he isn't one of the key scholars for the course.*

Understanding the Temple

It's not part of the specification, but you won't understand the conflicts within Judaism or the final days of Jesus' ministry unless you understand the role the Temple played in the Jewish religion of the 1st century

The original Temple was built by King David's son Solomon as a place to house the Ark of the Covenant. Over the centuries, Davidic kings of Judah tried to make the Jerusalem Temple the focal point of the national religion. However, in 586 BCE the Babylonians destroyed the Temple and the Kingdom of Judah too. The Ark vanished from history.

When the Babylonian Exiles returned to their homeland, they began building a new Temple, which was completed in 516 BCE. This was the "Second Temple". It was modeled on Solomon's Temple and was a relatively small building.

The priests of this new Temple held a lot of power. The 70 leading priests formed a parliament called the SANHEDRIN that met every day to rule on cases where the Jewish laws were broken. High Priests were appointed by kings and emperors - first the Seleucid kings, then the Hasmoneans and Herodians, eventually the Roman Emperors. Because they were political appointees - and appointed often by Gentiles and foreigners - they were widely distrusted by many Jews.

King Herod the Great, in a bid for fame and popularity, set about rebuilding and enlarging the Second Temple. He coated the walls with gold and built huge columned courtyards for worshipers. He intended the Temple to be one of the Wonders of the Ancient World. However, its association with Herod only tainted the Temple further in the eyes of many Jews.

What went on in the Temple? In a nutshell, animal sacrifice. The Old Testament instructs worshipers to sacrifice various types of animals to God. Ordinary Jews could visit the Temple and pay the priests a Temple Tax to sacrifice animals on their behalf, usually to remove a sin and make themselves pure before God. They were also expected to bring a sacrificial lamb during the Festival of Passover. The animals were killed then burnt on outdoor altars so the smoke could float into the sky. The roasted animal would then be eaten, either by the priests or the worshipers (as part of the Passover meal,in those days)..

This wasn't unusual in itself. All ancient pagan temples were sacred abattoirs too. What was unusual about the Jerusalem Temple was the sheer scale of the animal sacrifice that went on every day. Millions of animals were brought to the temple every year to be slaughtered.

Only 'unblemished' (physically perfect) animals could be sacrificed and selling these lambs and bulls and pigeons to worshipers was a profitable trade. The animal-sellers ran stores in the outer courtyard of the Temple.

In addition, Roman money couldn't be used inside the Temple, because it had pictures of the Emperor on it and he claimed to be a god. Worshipers had to pay the priests their Temple Tax in silver coins called shekels. Money changers operated in the outer courtyard, changing local currency into silver shekels (and making a tidy profit themselves).

A silver half shekel, as used to pay the Temple Tax

Weirdly, the silver shekel had pagan images on it too! Oh well, at least it didn't have the hated Roman emperor on it....

So what with the animal-sellers, the money-changers, the tour guide operator (yes, they had them too), the priests in their tall hats advising people on what sacrifices to offer and the gift shops selling souvenirs (yes, they had them too!), the outer courtyard of the temple was a crowded marketplace.

For some Jews, the Temple seemed to have become a profit-driven business run by politicians rather than a place devoted to the worship of God. Traveling to Jerusalem every year as a pilgrim and paying for a sacrificial lamb at Passover was expensive too - putting the central religious worship of 1st century Judaism outside the reach of many ordinary people.

Reconstruction of what Herod's Temple looked like

Jesus & the Temple

Jesus visited the Temple when he arrived in Jerusalem for Passover. He clearly didn't like what he saw going on. Jesus started a noisy protest, overturning the tables of the money-changers and driving out the animals with a whip. He accused the businessmen and priests of turning the Temple into "*a den of thieves*".

Jesus also made a surprising announcement, claiming, "*Destroy this Temple and I will raise it up in 3 days*" (**John 2: 19-20**). Jesus is taking about **himself** being the true Temple and predicting his Resurrection. However, these words came back to haunt Jesus. At his trial, witnesses were produced who claimed he had said that **he** planned to destroy the Temple (which would have been blasphemy and terrorism). Given the protest Jesus had made with the money-changers, it's understandable how he might have left the impression he wanted to see the Temple destroyed.

> *Some critics argue that the outer court was so huge that Jesus' protest can't have been more than a minor disturbance. Nonetheless, it clearly made a big impression on the people in charge!*

The Sadducees

The **Sadducees** were the most influential religious group among the Jews. They were from the aristocratic families of Judea and they were used to wealth and privilege. They had very conservative (old fashioned) attitudes on many matters. They based their religious beliefs entirely on the Torah (the first 5 books of the Old Testament) and they took the laws in these scriptures very literally. For this reason, they concerned themselves with maintaining the Temple in Jerusalem and carrying out sacrifices as detailed in the Old Testament.

The Sadducees controlled the political life of Judea. Not all Temple priests were Sadducees, but the majority was and so were most of the people on the Sanhedrin; almost all the High Priests in the 1st century were Sadducees. The Sadducees were very wealthy and saw the Temple as the source of their power and prestige. The High Priest during Jesus' lifetime was **Joseph Caiaphas**. Caiaphas had been High Priest for 18 years, which suggests he was well-connected and probably a Sadducee.

As religious conservatives, the Sadducees resisted **Hellenic influences** (p47) in the Jewish religion. They did not accept the Greek philosophical notion of the immortal soul and did not believe in life after death. They rejected the idea of a spirit world inhabited by angels and seem to have been quite sceptical about miracles. Some sources suggest they were **Deists**, believing that God does not intervene in history.

> *After the destruction of the Temple in 70 CE, the Sadducees disappear. Without the Temple and its daily sacrifices, their religious code had no meaning.*

Jesus & the Sadducees

The Sadducees came from the opposite end of Jewish society from Jesus and his Galilean followers. Jesus' teachings about life after death bring him into conflict with Sadducees, who ask him awkward questions about the Afterlife. Jesus responds by referring to Moses and the Burning Bush, which is in the Torah (the books of the Old Testament the Sadducees respected most) and argues that the Torah implies there is life after death.

John's Gospel describes an emergency meeting of the Sanhedrin after Jesus raises Lazarus from the dead. The Sadducees seem concerned that the Romans will close down the Temple and destroy the country if Jesus carries on. That seems a bit far-fetched

Although it turns out to be true: the Romans DID demolish the Temple when they invaded Judea in 70 CE after the Great Jewish Revolt, but hat had nothing to do with Jesus.

Possibly, the Sadducees were offended by stories that Jesus could raise the dead - which was impossible according to their beliefs.

These philosophical debates escalate into something more serious when Jesus comes to Jerusalem for Passover - and before the week is over the High Priest has arrested Jesus and put him on trial before the Sanhedrin. The charges against Jesus are that he threatened to destroy the Temple (which would have alarmed the Sadducees), but the main charge that offends High Priest Caiaphas is that Jesus claims to be the Messiah.

The Pharisees

The Pharisees were the group that opposed the Sadducees. They lacked the wealth and political connections, but they were numerous and much more popular among the ordinary people, especially in areas far away from the Temple, like Galilee.

However, the two groups weren't entirely opposed. There were Pharisees who were priests at the Temple and some Pharisees were members of the ruling Sanhedrin.

Whereas the Sadducees thought being a good Jew meant sticking to the rules in the Torah (first 5 books of the Old Testament) and keeping the sacrifices at the Temple going, the Pharisees taught a more personal sort of code. They had built up a huge body of teachings that went beyond the Torah, based on traditions, prophets and philosophizing. These laws covered every area of Jewish life, from eating and washing to working, sex and death. The Pharisees' intention wasn't to tie people up in petty rules (though it might feel like that at times), but to provide Jews with a complete code for living which they could adopt in the middle of a pagan world and still remain faithful to their ancient faith.

Since they incorporated teachings that went beyond the Torah, the Pharisees held a number of **Hellenic ideas** (p47, though they perhaps didn't see these ideas as being 'Greek'). They believed in the immortal soul and in life after death. They believed in a spirit world inhabited by angels. However, in other ways they were quite anti-Hellenic: they believed Judaism provided a complete way of life that was superior to what was offered by the surrounding pagan culture.

After the destruction of the Temple in 70 CE, the Pharisees gained a lot of authority. Pharisees backed Simon Bar Kokhbar's revolt against the Romans and proclaimed him to be the Messiah. After the Romans destroyed Jerusalem and scattered the Jewish population, Pharisees disappeared but many of their ideas passed into the Rabbinical Judaism that emerged later (and is still around today).

Jesus & the Pharisees

The Gospels show Jesus clashing with the Pharisees on many occasions. This makes sense, because Jesus travelled around ordinary Jewish towns like Capernaum and the Pharisees were the main religious group in Jewish society away from Jerusalem and the Temple.

Jesus condemns the Pharisees on many occasions for being spiritually proud. He accuses them of focusing too much on outward show of 'following the rules' and not enough on the inner state of loving God. He frequently calls them **HYPOCRITES**, meaning that they claim to stand for something good but in their private lives they are completely wicked.

Today, the word "pharisee" or "pharisaical" describes someone who is very arrogant and obsessed with imposing petty rules and regulations

Matthew's Gospel has particularly heated attacks on the Pharisees. Jesus pronounces a series of "*woes*" (curses) on the Pharisees and others like them who treat religion as a set of rules to follow. He calls them "*snakes*" and compares them to "*whitewashed tombs*" that look good on the outside but are rotten on the inside:

Jesus' criticisms come from the Pharisees' concern with PURITY. By following the rules of Phariseeism, Jews could keep themselves ritually pure or "clean". If they broke the rules, they became impure. It was important to keep yourself in a state of purity before God, so the rules could become more important than basic values like loving your neighbour. Keeping the rules successfully could lead to spiritual pride, the feeling that you are holier than anyone else. The Pharisees seem to have avoided the company of publicans and the sick, because these people were IMPURE or UNCLEAN. Women were also considered unclean and excluded from Pharisee worship and prayer.

Jesus rejected Pharisee notions of purity and impurity. He associated with publicans and women. He ministered to the sick and the dead. He freely broke rules like the Sabbath restrictions. In the **Parable of the Pharisee & the Publican**, Jesus shows that God prefers a humble publican to a proud Pharisee.

The idea that sincerely repenting your sins and throwing yourself on the mercy of God is more important than following religious rules goes straight to the heart of Jesus' disagreements with the Pharisees

However, Jesus also shared a lot in common with the Pharisees. He believed in many of the things they believed in: that faith was about more than sticking to the Torah and carrying out animal sacrifices in the Temple, that there was life after death. Some scholars argue that Jesus was himself a Pharisee (or a rogue Pharisee) and that his arguments with the Pharisees show that he was part of their group. Even the hostility in Jesus' arguments might show membership of this group because exaggerated arguments are part of the Jewish tradition of debate.

Two Pharisees are mentioned by name in the Gospels and both are influential members of the Sanhedrin. **Nicodemus** visits Jesus by night to learn his beliefs; **Joseph of Arimathea** also became a follower of Jesus. Both men are present at the Crucifixion and provide a burial for Jesus in a nearby tomb. This suggests that Jesus' relations with the Pharisees were not *entirely* hostile.

The Essenes

The Essenes were a much smaller Jewish sect. They completely rejected the Temple in Jerusalem and the animal sacrifices that went on there. But they also rejected living in the pagan world, among the Gentiles, and trying to remain ritually pure by sticking to Pharisaical laws. Instead, the Essenes withdrew from the world to live in separate communities. In effect, the Essenes were monks. The sect was found in the 2nd century BCE after the Maccabean Revolt and their writings refer to the sect being inspired by a 'Teacher of Righteousness' who opposes a 'Wicked Priest' who has led mainstream Jews astray. This reflects the Essene belief that the Temple cult led by the Sadducees had become corrupt.

The main Essene communities were out in the Judean desert, far away from corrupt civilisation. However, some Essenes seem to have lived in cities, presumably in 'monasteries' where they could live separately from everyone else. The Essenes were ASCETICS (they gave up worldly pleasure) and they held all their possessions in common; many Essenes were CELIBATE (they gave up sex) but there seem to have been some Essene groups that allowed marriage. They seem to have been pacifists, but they carried weapons to defend themselves from bandits when traveling.

The interesting Essene practice is BAPTISM: a ritual washing away of sins. It seems the Essenes did this daily and preferred to be fully immersed in water (not just sprinkle it on their heads). This leads some scholars to wonder if John the Baptist was an Essene - or a rogue Essene leader who started his own movement. All four Gospels describe John the Baptist living an ascetic lifestyle in the desert and baptizing huge crowds in the River Jordan. However, John didn't seem to expect his followers to join a monastery or share his ascetic lifestyle.

The Essenes looked forward to two Messiahs (or perhaps one Messiah with two functions). A Priestly Messiah would restore pure worship to the Jews; a Kingly Messiah would lead a war against pagans and free the Jews from oppression.

The Essenes probably viewed themselves as getting back to a "pure" form of Judaism, but ironically their beliefs and practices were probably influenced by **Hellenism** (p47). Ancient Judaism didn't support celibacy or withdrawing from the world. This asceticism instead resembles the Cynic philosophy of the Greeks.

After the destruction of the Temple in 70 CE, the Essenes also faded from history. Without the Temple-cult to oppose, they probably lost their main reason for existing. Also, the Romans seem to have hunted down and destroyed Essene communities in case they were supporting the Zealots.

One of these communities was Qumran near the Dead Sea. The people there hid their library in nearby caves and this library - the Dead Sea scrolls - was discovered in the 1940s, incredibly intact. The DSS show us the earliest versions of the Old Testament and shed some light on the beliefs of the Essenes.

Jesus & the Essenes

The Bible never mentions the Essenes, but could Jesus have been one? **Barbara Thiering** proposes that Jesus could have been the 'Teacher of Righteousness' described in the Dead Sea Scrolls.

There are problems with Thiering's view. The 'Teacher of Righteousness' would have lived over a hundred years before Jesus' time. But more importantly, the Essenes cut themselves off from the sinful world and kept their purity by living an ascetic lifestyle - whereas Jesus went to the towns of Galilee and to Jerusalem, he went to weddings, he drank wine and attended dinner parties and associated with publicans and other impure people.

On the other hand, Jesus begins his Ministry by being baptized by **John the Baptist**. Jesus' disciples baptized people too. This sounds like an Essene ritual. Moreover, if John the Baptist was an Essene, then if Jesus went to be baptized by John, he must have spent at least *some* time among the Essenes and been sympathetic to their beliefs and practices.

Furthermore, Jesus goes out into the desert to pray and fast for 40 days and night in the famous passage where he is tempted by the Devil. This sort of 'religious retreat' into the Judean desert seems to have been a common thing for religious 1st century Jews - and it seems that such retreats took place at Essene monasteries in the desert. Readers of the Bible often assume that Jesus was alone in the desert, but the Gospels don't say that. It would have been more normal for a pilgrim to go to a desert community to pray and fast alongside the Essenes.

Another interesting link comes from the **John's Gospel**, which frequently refers to Jesus as the Light of the World. The Light/Dark motif used to be viewed by scholars as a sign of **Hellenic influence** (p47) in John's Gospel rather than the teaching of a genuine 1st century Jew - in other words, John added this symbolism in but Jesus never really spoke that way.

However, the DSS (Dead Sea Scrolls) reveal that the Essenes referred to themselves as "*Children of the Light*" and the pagans and sinful Jews as "*Children of the Darkness*". So perhaps John's Gospel *does* preserve the way Jesus spoke, using symbolism inspired by the Essenes.

The Zealots

Josephus refers to the Zealots as a "*fourth philosophy*" after the Sadducees, Pharisees and Essenes. The Zealots were a military sect, dedicated to freeing the Jews from Roman occupation by violence. Josephus claims the Zealots were founded in 6 CE, when an uprising was led by Judas of Galilee and a priest named Zadok. However, violent religious fanatics date back before this and the Zealots probably emerged during the Maccabean Revolt in the 2nd century BCE. In the 1st century, the Zealots particularly objected to paying taxes to Rome.

The Zealots were probably a diverse lot. Some of them might have been gangs of bandits who justified their criminal activities with religious claims, but others were genuine freedom fighters who expected a **Kingly Messiah** to lead them in their war against the Roman Empire; most of the time they engaged in guerrilla warfare. Some times their targets were other Jews, like the publicans and the Sadducees who collaborated with the Roman regime. Josephus mentions the *sicarii* ("dagger-men") who would hide knives in their robes, mingle with crowds and assassinate Jewish enemies - or even random strangers, in an attempt to spread terror. In 56 CE, they assassinated High Priest Jonathan, right in the middle of the Temple.

The existence of the Zealots explains why the Romans were so nervous about uprisings. Any popular leader who attracted huge crowds was potentially a Zealot recruiter - and large crowds attracted the *sicarii* to do their indiscriminate killings.

The Zealots had their moment in 66 CE. Protests against taxes turned into a full scale rebellion that swept the Romans out of Judea. A Jewish government was created in Jerusalem, with many Zealots in top positions. The Romans returned and in 70 CE, Jerusalem was captured. The Temple was demolished. The Zealots had a last stand at the desert fortress of Masada. In 73 CE, these Zealots committed mass suicide rather than surrender to the Romans.

Jesus & the Zealots

Obviously, Jesus was completely opposed to the Zealots' violent philosophy. Jesus urged his followers to put away weapons and respond to violence with peace:

> *But I tell you, do not resist an evil person. If anyone slaps you on the right cheek, turn to them the other cheek also* - **Matthew 5: 39**

Jesus is questioned on his attitude to paying tax. The Gospels present this question as a 'trap' - if Jesus urges Jews not to pay taxes he is siding with the Zealots but if he supports the Romans then he is an enemy of the Jewish people. Jesus answers carefully, saying that people should give God what God demands (worship and moral living) and give money but not worship to Caesar.

However, one of Jesus' Twelve Disciples was **Simon the Zealot**. Why would Jesus recruit a Zealot to his group? Scholars propose that Simon the Zealot was recruited to balance Matthew the Tax Collector (publican). These were two people who should hate each other, so their working together would demonstrate the love and forgiveness that Jesus taught exists in the **Kingdom of God**.

Another Disciple was **Judas Iscariot**, who betrayed Jesus. There are many theories about what the name 'Iscariot' means, but one theory is that it means *sicarius* - so Judas was one of the extremist *sicarii* dagger-men. However, this translation isn't certain and Josephus claims the *sicarii* only appeared in the 50s CE, a couple of decades **after** Jesus.

R.F. Brandon argues that Judas was a Zealot assassin and Jesus was a revolutionary political leader who everyone expected would raise an army against Rome. However, Jesus (wisely) rejected a violent revolution, realising military uprisings were doomed, and embraced pacifism instead. Brandon thinks this is why Judas betrayed him - for abandoning the Zealot cause. This is a colourful interpretation, but there's not enough evidence to support it.

What seems more certain is that the Romans **mistook** Jesus' movement for a gang of Zealots. Jesus was crucified between two other prisoners, described as *lestai* by Mark and Matthew - a word sometimes translated as "thieves" but really meaning "rebels". The same word is used to describe **Barabbas**, the "*notorious prisoner*" being tried at the same time as Jesus for his part in an "*uprising*". The Gospels describe the Roman governor Pontius Pilate releasing Barabbas rather than Jesus at the insistence of a mob.

Can we understand Jesus better by viewing him in the context of these Jewish groups?

YES

As a member of the royal Davidic line, Jesus belongs to the class the Sadducees came from, but his opposition to the Temple suggests he was inspired by the Essenes, as does his connection to John the Baptist and habit of retreating into the desert for fasting and prayer. Jesus specifically opposed the legalism of the Pharisees but shared their debating techniques. His enemies persuaded the Romans that he was a Zealot.

Even if Jesus is the Son of God, he has a human and a divine nature. Jesus' humanity will be formed like all human nature, through social relationships and as part of a community. This means that even if Jesus' teachings are divinely inspired, they will have a human side too inspired by the people Jesus knew growing up: certainly the Pharisees and possibly the Essenes too.

NO

Jesus is the Son of God and his teaching comes directly from God, not from any human source. Jesus says of himself "*the son can do nothing by himself; he can do only what he sees his father doing, because whatever the father does the son also does*" (John 5: 19). Therefore it's a mistake to try to understand Jesus by looking at the flawed or corrupt religious groups surrounding him.

The four sects or philosophies in 1st century Judaism were all destroyed before the century ended: they disappeared after the Temple was destroyed in 70 CE. We now know very little about them, except for (probably biased) passages in Josephus. Whereas Jesus' teachings have lasted 2000 years and are witnessed in all four Gospels. The best way to understand Jesus is with reference to the Bible, not Jewish sects.

KEY SCHOLARS

Raymond E Brown

Topic: 1.1 Prophecy regarding the Messiah

Raymond E Brown (1928-1998) is an American Roman Catholic priest and Bible scholar whose work features in other topics in this course too (**2.2 Titles of Jesus, 2.3 Miracles & Signs** and **3.2 Purpose & Authorship of the Fourth Gospel**).

Brown's contribution to this topic comes largely through his last book *Birth of the Messiah* (1998). This massive work examines the birth narratives in Matthew and Luke in close detail. Even though he's a Roman Catholic scholar, Brown's research and even-handedness make this a book Protestant Christians will refer to as well.

However, Brown is a liberal Christian and questions some of the beliefs Christians have taken for granted over the years. He regards the Bible as a human document, not a divine book. He interprets the birth narratives as works of fiction, created by the Gospelists to tell stories that reflect their beliefs about Jesus. For example, Matthew communicates his beliefs about Jesus being the Messiah, the 'new Moses' and the Son of David and writes to reassure Gentile Christians that the Messiah is important to them. Brown calls the Matthean birth narrative *"an attractive drama that catches the imagination."*

An example of the **Matthew's birth-narrative** (p30) being a human document would be the famous proof-text in Isaiah about a virgin conceiving and giving birth. Brown identifies the Hebrew word "*almah*" to describe the mother: *almah* means "young woman" but not necessarily a virgin; Hebrew has another word, "*bethulah*", which means a virgin. However, when the Old Testament was translated into Greek, *almah* was translated as "*parthenos*", a Greek word which definitely means 'virgin'. Matthew used the Greek Old Testament and may have misunderstood what Isaiah had been saying.

An example of the birth narrative appealing to different audiences and 'catching the imagination' would be Matthew's genealogy (family tree) which links Jesus back to Abraham as well as King David. Matthew's Jewish audience would be interested in Jesus' descent from King David but a Gentile (non-Jewish) audience would be more interested in Abraham, because God had promised a descendant of Abraham would bring a blessing to "*all peoples on earth*"- including the Gentiles. Jesus is therefore the promised Messiah for **both** groups.

Because of his liberal views on how Matthew's birth narrative came to be written, Brown's conclusions are rejected by fundamentalist and some conservative Christians. These groups regard the Bible as INERRANT (without error). These Christian readers try to HARMONISE the discrepancies between the birth narratives and genealogies in Matthew and Luke into a single story. They also take the Virgin Birth literally and interpret the Old Testament prophecies in a **futurist** sense as referring to the birth of Jesus rather than the events of 600-700 years before.

Morna Hooker

Topic: 1.1 Prophecy regarding the Messiah

Morna Hooker (b. 1938) is a Professor at Cambridge University and a Bible scholar whose work also features in another topic in this course **(2.1 Prologue in John)**.

Hooker wrote a slim introduction to New Testament scholarship called **Beginnings: Keys that Open the Gospels** (1998). It's a very readable book and available cheap from online booksellers so I'd recommend it for students. She argues that each Gospel has a prologue that works as a "*key*" to "*unlock*" the main themes and teachings about Jesus. Matthew's describes the circumstances of Jesus' birth in Bethlehem and how his family ended up living in Nazareth in Galilee. Hooker calls Matthew's Prologue the "*prophetic key*" because it focuses on Jesus as the Messiah and 'second Moses' predicted by the Old Testament prophets.

Much of Hooker's career has been taken up with arguing against various theories that try to construct a 'historical Jesus' that is different from the Jesus Christ of Christian faith. In **The Gospel According to St Mark** (1993), Hooker demolishes Wilhelm Wrede's famous theory of the **Messianic Secret** (p23). Hooker argues against Wrede, and claims that that the descriptions of Jesus being called the Messiah are historical and were not invented later by Christians. Hooker thinks it is plausible that Jesus would have tried to 'play down' his identity as the promised Messiah, because it was too politically explosive and would have distracted from his mission. She says, "'if he believed himself to be in any sense the Messiah, the last thing he would do was to claim the title for himself".

> In **Topic 3.1**, you will learn how Wrede's theory is part of Redaction Criticism and Hooker's response to it is part of a backlash against this approach to interpreting the texts of the New Testament.

However, Hooker is not a conservative Christian scholar. In her first book, **Jesus & the Servant** (1959), she argues against the view the Suffering Servant in **Isaiah's Servant Songs** (p17) is supposed to predict Jesus. Hooker goes through Isaiah's "Servant Songs" line by line and then goes through the synoptic Gospels (Matthew, Mark and Luke) line by line, looking for links but does not find a definite connection. She ends up placing the Servant Songs within the framework of Isaiah as a whole, arguing the message can be summed up as: "*Israel, who has been chosen by Yahweh as his servant, is to be restored from Exile and will manifest God's glory to all nations*". In other words, the Servant represents the Jewish nation collectively, not the future Messiah. This is an unpopular view with people who think Isaiah is specifically predicting the death and Resurrection of Jesus, but it links her to **Raymond E. Brown** who also interprets Old Testament prophecies in a preterist rather than a futurist sense.

GLOSSARY OF TERMS

Atoning Death: A death that makes up for sins

Babylonian Exile: Lasting from 597 BCE to 539 BCE, the **Jews** of **Judea** were taken into exile in Babylonia (modern Iraq) after their kingdom was destroyed

Bethlehem: Small village 5 miles south of **Jerusalem**; birth place of **David** and of the **Messiah** according to the **prophecy** of Micah

David: Greatest king of a united **Israel** who reigned around 1000 BCE; the descendants of David ruled **Judah** until the **Babylonian Exile**; the **Messiah** is descended from David

Essenes: Jewish sect that retreated to the desert to await the **Messiah** and opposed the cult of the **Temple** run by the **Sadducees**

Futurist: Interpreting a **prophecy** so that it refers to events in the future or at the end of the world

Galilee: Region to the north of **Judea** consisting of wooded hills and farmland surrounding Lake Galilee; an agricultural community with a mixture of **Jews** and **Gentiles**

Genealogy: A family tree showing a person's ancestors

Gentile: Someone who isn't **Jewish** by birth

Hellenism: The Greek culture of the Roman Empire, especially its pagan religion, philosophy and art

Herod: King of a wider Judea from 37 BCE to 4 BCE; infamous for his massacres and murders but also his grand building projects; known as Herod "the Great"

Isaiah: Prophet who lived in **Jerusalem** around 700 BCE at the time of the fall of the Kingdom of **Israel**; also the Book of the Old Testament believed to be written by him

Israel: the united kingdom ruled by **David** around 1000 BCE; also the name of the northern kingdom after the break-up of David's kingdom that lasted until the Assyrians invaded in 722 BCE; can also refer to the entire **Jewish** nation collectively because Israel was the name of their ancestor

Jerusalem: Capital city of **David**, later the capital of the Kingdom of **Judah**; home to the **Temple** and centre of Jewish culture

Jew: A person who follows the Jewish religion and is born into a Jewish family descended from the Old Testament children of **Israel**

Judah: Southern kingdom with **Jerusalem** as its capital and ruled by the line of **David** that endured until the **Babylonian Exile**

Judea: Kingdom of **Herod** (including **Galilee**); after his death a smaller province (not including Galilee) ruled by a Roman governor

Messiah: The Anointed One; predicted saviour or king in Judaism (*Christos* in Greek)

Messianic Secret: Theory of Wilhelm Wrede that Jesus never claimed to be the **Messiah** and that Mark's Gospel treats his Messiah-ship as a secret

Pharisees: Jewish sect concerned with obeying the Law in every aspect of life; represented as in conflict with the first Christians

Preterist: Interpreting a **prophecy** so that it refers to events occurring in the lifetime of the prophet

Proof Text: The use of an Old Testament **prophecy** to link with an event in Jesus' life and prove that he is the **Messiah**

Prophecy: A statement (often in the form of poetry) that reveals the will of God to humans

Publican: A **Jew** who collaborates with the Roman Empire by helping the Romans collect taxes from other Jews

Sadducees: Jewish sect that ran the **Temple** and collaborated with the Romans

Suffering Servant: A character who appears in the Book of **Isaiah** who serves God loyally but is tortured by his enemies; may represent either the **Jewish** nation or Jesus

Temple: Central place of Jewish worship in **Jerusalem**; originally built by **David**'s son Solomon around 950 BCE but destroyed by the Babylonians in 597 BCE; the Second Temple was built after the **Babylonian Exile** and expanded by **Herod** but destroyed by the Romans in 70 CE

Zealots: Jewish sect that believed in armed revolt against the Roman occupation

ABOUT THE AUTHOR

Jonathan Rowe is a teacher of Religious Studies, Psychology and Sociology at Spalding Grammar School and he creates and maintains the **www.psychologywizard.net** site for Edexcel A-Level Psychology. He has worked as an examiner for various Exam Boards but is not affiliated with Edexcel. This series of books grew out of the resources he created for his students. Jonathan also writes novels and creates resources for his hobby of fantasy wargaming. He likes warm beer and smooth jazz.

28615677R00042

Printed in Great Britain
by Amazon